AN
UNCOMMON
CORRESPONDENCE

AN
UNCOMMON
CORRESPONDENCE

An East-West Conversation

on Friendship, Intimacy and Love

IVY GEORGE & MARGARET MASSON

PAULIST PRESS • New York / Mahwah, N.J.

The Publisher gratefully acknowledges use of the poem "Out of the Blue" by Micheal O'Siadhail. Used by permission of Bloodaxe Books, Ltd.

Jacket design and book design by Cynthia Dunne

Library of Congress Cataloging-in-Publication Data

George, Ivy.
　　　An uncommon correspondence : an East-West conversation on friendship, intimacy, and love / by Ivy George and Margaret Masson.
　　　　　p.　　cm.
　　　ISBN 0–8091–0500–4 (alk. paper)
　　　　　1. Love. 2. Intimacy (Psychology). 3. Female friendship.
4. George, Ivy—Correspondence. 5. Women college teachers—20th century—Correspondence. 6. Masson, Margaret, 1961—Correspondence. 7. Women sociologists—20th century—Correspondence. I. Masson, Margaret, 1961– . II. Title.
BF575. L8G46　1998　　　　　　　　　98-8520
158.2—dc21　　　　　　　　　　　　　CIP

Published by Paulist Press
997 Macarthur Boulevard
Mahwah, New Jersey 07430

www.paulistpress.com

Printed and bound in the
United States of America

Distributed in the UK by
C. Goodliffe Neal LTD/Fowler Wright Books
Arden Forest Industrial Estate
Warwickshire B49 6ER
England

FAX 01789764343
Phone 01789763261

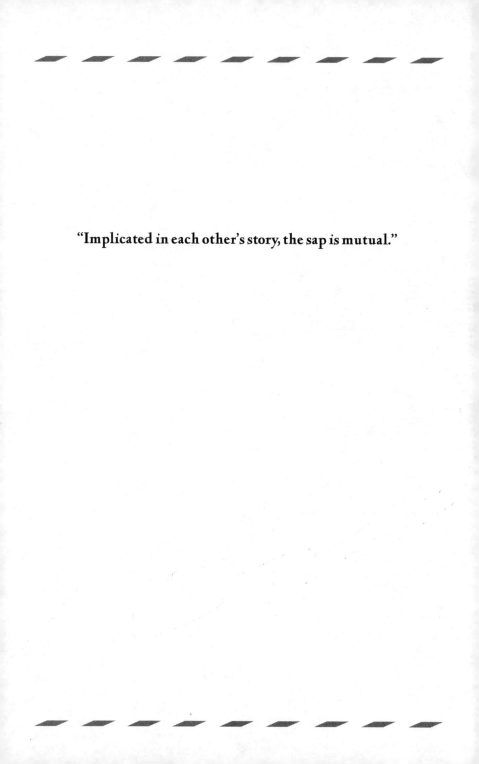

"Implicated in each other's story, the sap is mutual."

TABLE OF CONTENTS

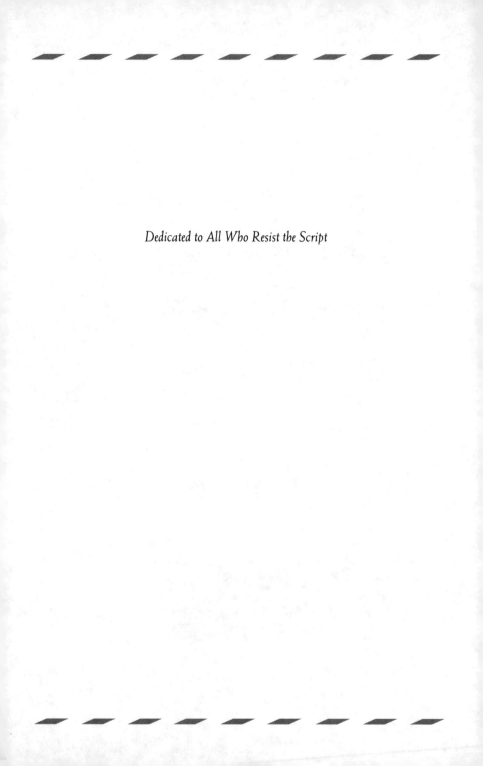

Dedicated to All Who Resist the Script

ACKNOWLEDGMENTS

All writers are indebted to innumerable intangible sources. Yet, there are a few individuals whose names we are able to acknowledge explicitly.

For their readings of our letters and for their thoughtful editorial suggestions, we are deeply grateful to Robert Song, Ruth Etchells and Stephen Barton. Thanks also go to Nancy Linton, Director of the Women's May Term Program at the Oregon Extension of Houghton College, the faculty there and the wonderful groups of students who used the manuscript and commented on it over many sessions.

Then there are those who believed in the project, and supported us with their enthusiasm and inspired us of its worth. Among these stand Robert Song, Michael Vasey, Preston and Connie Williams, Sean Lennox, Virginia Sohn, Howard Richardson, Diana Peck, Sue Ackermann, Claire and Nicholas Wolterstorff, John Thomas and most of all our late and beloved Aunt Margaret. And without Abraham Philip there may well have been no book....

We are also immensely grateful to our friend Micheal O'Siadhail for permission to use his poem "Out of the Blue."

We thank Paulist Press and our editor Kathleen Walsh for supporting this project and sending it along its way.

And of course we are grateful to each other. The memories of two Christmas holidays when we took our turns in the study and rapidly processed each other's work are testimony to a special conviviality in an ongoing friendship that takes new shapes every day.

AN
UNCOMMON
CORRESPONDENCE

OUT OF THE BLUE

[Micheal O'Siadhail]

Nothing can explain this adventure—let's say a quirk
of fortune steered us together—we made our covenants,
began this odyssey of ours, by hunch and guesswork,
a blind date where foolish love consented in advance.
No my beloved, neither knew what lay behind the frontiers.
You told me once you hesitated: A needle can waver,
then fix on its pole; *I am still after many years*
baffled that the needle's gift dipped in my favour.
Should I dare to be so lucky? Is this a dream?
Suddenly in the commonplace that first amazement seizes
me all over again—a freak twist to the theme,
subtle jazz of the new familiar, trip of surprises.
Gratuitous, beyond our fathom, both binding and freeing,
this love re-invades us, shifts the boundaries of our being.

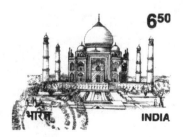

INTRODUCTION

Margaret Masson

This is a book about love. It is a cross-cultural exploration of certain modes of human intimacy—courtship, friendship, celibacy, marriage—and grows out of the cultural traditions of both East and West. It is grounded in an attempt to find a resting place on the edges of the choppy waters of human passions, and from there to discover a more reflective, constructive, directed means of negotiating the powerful rapids of human sexuality. Written in the form of a series of letters, it is a conversation between two women from different cultures who became close friends: one grew up in India and moved to the United States as a young adult; the other is a Scottish woman who spent her childhood in Zambia, her adolescence in Scotland and her early adulthood between the United States and England. It is an endeavour which began, like so many things, almost by accident, its roots drawing silent sap from their fortuitous friendship. . . .

Few friendships change lives. Perhaps, for most of us, we find two or three people, if we are lucky, whose friendship "shifts the boundaries of our being." On a dull fall day in Michigan in 1987, I first set eyes on one such friend. It was a busy Sunday morning service and, as separate newcomers, we found no opportunity to talk. But we had noticed each other, as strangers and sojourners often do: she, a small striking Indian woman, I, a tall, pale Britisher, both of us, as I recall, unmissable on that grey Michigan morning in the dazzling colour of our respective attire.

It was a couple of days later when we were invited out to tea together that I realised that Ivy George could be one of those boundary-shifting friends in my life. Some people tell of how they knew at once, on meeting someone for the very first time, that this person would be the love of their life. I had something of that intuition with Ivy: it was a kind of "falling into friendship," with the same sense of inevitability and gratitude— "Should I dare to be so lucky?"—that people often feel when they are falling in love. It was not and has never been an "in love" set of emotions (how paltry is our modern vocabulary for describing friendship) but the same thankfulness that some quirk of fortune had steered us to this unlikely place so far from our respective homes at the same time remains with me. Even now, years later, when the friendship has matured and endured the trials and tribulations to which all friendships are prone, I wince at the thought that with a slight adjustment here (a different year), an invitation unproffered there, I might never even have known that she existed. Lovers often know this shiver at the unthinkable missing. Friends may know it too.

When we first met, I had just become a professor of English in a Midwestern college in the United States, and Ivy, a sociologist, was to be the college's multicultural fellow for the year. I was twenty-eight, she was thirty-three. Her vivacity at our first meeting was, I later discovered, partly on account of a promising suitor she was preparing to meet: a brilliant young Indian doctor was about to fly in from the neighbouring city and Ivy felt that this was the first man in a while who sounded like a real possibility. The next time we met, she was crestfallen. Within a very short time of their meeting, she had known that this was not the man for her, and it was in her loneliness then that she began to unfold her private drama in a way that intrigued and fascinated me. Yet it also gave me a glimpse into the cost of the struggle to shift the boundaries of one's culture.

This insight into the way someone from another culture played the game of love was not only intriguing, it was also to have an important impact on my own assumptions and perspectives. As I watched my friend picking her way (sometimes resigned, sometimes rebellious) through the network of family obligation, personal desire and cultural dictates that makes up an "arranged marriage," the inevitability of my own expectations and experiences was called into question. As I stumbled through a series of relationships and infatuations with the usual hopes and heartbreaks of a young Western woman, I now found myself with something more than a sympathetic friend. Ivy was no mirror image. She was not someone who would ease my heartache with empathetic nods of "I've been there too." Here was a friend who had grown up with a different set of cultural norms, a different set of expectations and values when it came to matters of the heart. Frequently, I was offered not just a shoulder to cry on, but also a radically alternative perspective—and if this was sometimes disturbing, it was as often to prove, ultimately, profoundly liberating.

After our year in the Midwest, Ivy returned to the East Coast and I eventually moved back to England. The friendship continued to flourish at a distance, often sustained by long letters across the ocean. These chronicled the time of Ivy's courtship and marriage and my own periods of wrestling with some of the imponderables thrown before young Westerners in early adulthood. Sometimes, one of us would share extracts from these letters with friends traversing similar ground; often they found it helpful simply knowing they were not alone; sometimes it was even possible to learn from another's mistakes and discoveries.

While our letters told two different and particular stories, we also recognised at some deeper level that the experiences recounted were not uniquely our own. The patterns echoed the narratives of countless others;

the issues and dilemmas were common fare. It was in this spirit that we decided to attempt something more public, more comprehensive, more focused. We hoped that readers might draw encouragement and comfort (and, no doubt, wry amusement) from glimpses into experiences not so very different from their own. We also hoped that the vantage point provided by our dialogue—this conversation which takes place across and between cultures—would offer readers what it has offered us: a means of stepping aside for a while from the "inevitabilities" of one's own culture and a perspective from which to reconsider and reflect, to weigh and ponder, amidst the dizzying eddies of emotion, which streams to float with, which currents to resist. Perhaps in the sharing of a part of our own struggles and joys, others might find here the opportunity to engage with these common issues and discover a foothold in the reeds, something to hold onto against the river's insistent undertow.

In this book, we tell the story of a significant year of our lives, and, through these interweaving narratives, we explore some of the contemporary dilemmas for those seeking intimacy amidst the rapidly changing expectations of today's global culture. We examine the modern compulsion towards romantic love and how individuals cope with the dictates of tradition and culture from an East-West perspective. We consider the alternatives available for human intimacy other than romance. What of singleness, celibacy, friendship and homosexuality? We discuss various forms of courtship and their social implications for the institutions of marriage and family, and gender relations, and we conclude with a view of intimacy beyond the altar, as it relates to new relationships inside and outside the bonds of marriage.

What follows is a revised and edited version of our correspondence over about a year or so. We discussed many things, political and cultural as well as personal in our letters. For the purposes of this book, we have picked out only the strands which offer a glimpse into our struggle to find a better way of loving by testing and even trying to transcend the boundaries of our respective cultures.

Although the book is written by two women, it is of course informed by a perspective wider than just the female. Conversations with male friends have also shaped the thinking here. Men, no less than women, are searching for intimacy, for new and more authentic ways of relating. We hope that they, too, will find echoes of their own search here.

Such a venture is risky. It is one thing to share with friends one's failures and foibles when it comes to matters of the heart. In public print, one feels very exposed, and we are well aware of the dangers of narcissism, exhibitionism and other kinds of self-indulgence. And yet, we are persuaded that the project is worthwhile. If this book helps the reader in his or her quest towards a reevaluation, we shall be deeply glad. We have altered some names and circumstances in order to protect the privacy of others—and our own. However, the experiences remain true to our lives.

PART ONE

Romantic Love, Inevitably

Another Failed Romance

England: 15th January 1989

Dear Ivy,

    I must have a sabbatical from men! Now that I'm back on home turf, I can't believe that I nearly continued that relationship with Brad. I know it was an unlikely prospect from the beginning: there was such a slim chance of discovering in him a truly kindred spirit. I was aware at the outset that we had a very different sense of what life might be all about and that the promise of any depth of intimacy could only be meagre. And yet why did I wait and hope, putting up with so much dishonesty along the way? Was I so desperate for love that I was indeed blind? So yearning for intimacy that I was easily fooled—and by myself much more than I ever was by him? How could I have been so stupid? I am really grateful for your help in making me see sense, even though it took a while. Now I really wonder why. I suppose it was partly that I was flattered by his pursuit, enjoying the attention, the sense of being special to someone, of being found intriguing, attractive, desirable. It was so good to hold someone's hand again, to be held again, to be kissed, after what has seemed like so very long.

Right from the start I probably knew that we were mismatched, but such was my desire to be "in a relationship" again (the exclusivity of the phrase is striking, as if love affairs constitute *the* only category of relationship) that I deliberately rationalised all doubts. My justification for plunging in regardless? That at least I was being honest about it; I wasn't trying to pretend anything I didn't feel; and that the man was too emotionally shallow to suffer any pain anyhow. A cruel comment? Well, I'm angry! Yet again I get hurt and yet again I feel a fool for letting myself get involved in a relationship that was destined to cause each of us pain and disillusion. And this time, I don't feel in the mood to try and "redeem what was good." How much more self-knowledge of a certain kind does one need?

I know I'm not the only one who feels caught out by my emotions, seduced by my longing for love, trapped by what seems like a gambler's reckless compulsion to have another go, hoping against hope that this time is bound to be the winner. Maybe this new phase in my life, transplanted back into my native soil, regrafted into a familiar network, will give me some time and space to do some hard thinking. I really don't quite trust my own judgment any more. Increasingly, I realise how shaped I am by the compulsions of my culture; equally, I long for a way to transcend it—or at least not feel like such a victim of its seductive dictates, its empty promises and illusory dreams.

It has been a cold return. And yet I am glad to be here. I'm trying—time-honoured cure for broken hearts—to lose myself in my work. There's plenty of it and it is actually rather intriguing (two new courses to prepare), so my poor wounded heart can get on with its mending whilst the rest of me hopefully gets on with doing something useful. The beauty of this city is a real balm: I do so hope you can visit before too long. Simply living in the shadow of an ancient cathedral is somehow good for the spirit. One's sense of perspective is subtly changed by it. Countless lives through hundreds of years have already been lived out here; innumerable souls have struggled here to work out their various salvations, continuing in all the ambiguity of tradition. And the faith goes on, and lives go on, the same and yet always new.

It was a good five years in the States; being back here in England again, I realise how the experience has changed me: my world is that little bit bigger, perspectives have shifted, and I look at my own culture with more distance. I find myself drawn to others at one remove from the centre, not quite at the heart of the mainstream. That's no doubt why you and I became friends, drawn to each other by this shared sense of dissonance. I miss the fact that you are not a part of this world. And yet being back in a place that I can more easily feel is "home," the missing is less acute, somehow. Rootedness takes the edge off our vulnerability.

And yet, how I wish I could talk to you right now! More than anyone else I know, you shake me out of my cultural complacency, and I find myself questioning what I had assumed was universally true. It's disconcerting and sometimes disturbing, yes. But there is also something quite liberating about it. And, God knows, I need some liberation just now. I feel so locked into ways of relating that I feel powerless to resist; I suppose talking with you so often opens up new options, helps me find new ways of seeing and understanding and so saves me from feeling helplessly tossed and thrown about by some huge, irresistible cultural system I can but vaguely recognise and am powerless to direct. But maybe the fact that we can't talk now without it costing an arm and a leg across the ocean will force us into some sort of deeper exploration on paper.

What do you think, Ivy? Will you write me long letters, as if we had an evening or two to spend together? I am eager to hear your thoughts and experiences on these troublesome matters. I know we have talked countless times before, but it seems that my present circumstances—my recent romantic disaster and the relative security of being on home turf once more—create a space in which I feel the need to take stock. This Western compulsion towards romance: is it inevitable?

And yet I know that it is not—your own story proves this. How have you, how do you survive? How were your own instincts and desires shaped and directed? There must be a better way of relating than the present way of the West, and I so much want to find an alternative...before hurtling into the next fruitless infatuation. You see! I even write like a lemming! Be in touch soon, Ivy. I miss you, and am waiting to hear.

Love,
Margaret

An Indian Alternative

Dear Margaret,

Many thanks for your much awaited letter. I am well and busy, but I miss you very much. Your absence is made tolerable even slightly, celebrated by the knowledge that you have gone to a place that will restore you and nourish you in ways that a migrant's existence does not. I wonder how the future will shape up for you. Yet it was our mutual meanderings that brought us together, and for that I am deeply grateful.

You are very right—while the phone has its uses, letters have their own, especially on matters that are not particular events, but which still sit with us and shade so much of our doing and being every day. I am quite taken by the questions you raise; they are key questions in the lives of so many people. Matters of intimacy, dating and mating seem to plague people. I think of the students I work with, many of my friends and my own self, whose days are punctuated by the seasons of suitors. Many lives are altered by these questions—transforming them almost immutably. While my own life is not quite defined by these pressures to the same extent, nevertheless they prevail as a persistent reference to my being. I know that the quest for intimacy is universal, but I am also struck by the vast differences in the cultural means available for this quest. I am often intrigued by Western sensibilities in this matter and would be very interested in taking up your suggestion of exploring these matters in our correspondence. Telephone cost considerations may turn out to be a blessing as we put our pens to paper more deliberately. Your new start, reflective frame of mind and slightly more leisurely existence might give us the perfect opportunity to pick up the threads of scores of conversations and think together more systematically about some of these things.

Margaret, you raise many questions about "love," far more than I can begin to address here. So, let me start with your final questions—about my own shaping influences in this area. I find that in remarkable ways my culture and personal circumstances put me almost in direct opposition to your present position. Although ironically it was the lure of "relationships" that drove me from the inevitable destiny of marriage that I faced in India. As I have told you many times, I, like many of my friends, was captivated by the love stories of my youth. Denise Robbins, Barbara Cartland and Mills & Boon series were the staples of my teen summers. I found the attractions gripping and thought that surely I deserved to be a protagonist in an affair so lovely. Now that I live in the West, I am able to see even more sharply perhaps that culture has a tremendous impact on all our choices, much as we try to be critical of its sway. As I read your letter I was keenly aware that my own cultural expectations would not permit me the course you've been on. Yet, what appears to be striking is that there is something ineluctable about both our choices. Marriage and relationships are unalterably inscribed into both our social scripts. No doubt this is a universal aspect of human-social evolution.

I think of myself and my own future. Somehow the days ahead hold some promise and excitement for you—new place, new people, new opportunities. I am not so sure for myself. I have been here in the U.S. much longer than you were and quite possibly will stay here much longer than I plan to. I think of the circumstances of my leaving home and the reasons for coming here. I am not sure if I've told you how terrified I was when my bosom friends in India were taken away in what are called "arranged marriages"—when family and parents are involved in the selection of your partner. The girls seemed so young, having barely taken leave of their adolescence. Clearly, the dark clouds closing in on my friends (or what seemed to me dark anyhow) and the real fear of my own imminent capture drove me to take shelter in the world of romance, where one day some smashing, hirsute, stranger would come tapping on my waiting shoulder and confess undying love for me and only me. I'd read enough of those stories to start believing them. Surely these romances were the stuff of another reality, a wonderful world outside my orbit, and I desperately wanted a part of that. In my youthful confidence I wanted to take responsibility for my marriage and did not want to leave it to the designs of family and friends. More than that the idea of *choosing* and being *chosen exclusively* and *to be ever happy* was something to live for, yes even leave for.

I have a recurring dream ever since I left India. Every time, I wake up unnerved and wistful. Every time, it is the same scene: the faces of friends I knew in my convent school. The dream is a still life of all our girlish faces in our starched white uniforms, red ties, plaits in red ribbons. I wake up wishing more than anything to somehow reconnect with each one—even then knowing that each has disappeared into a life of marital and maternal mystery.

I don't know what happened to me; how I escaped the fate. Perhaps my maverick mother was an influence (much to her chagrin probably) or my indulgent father. Perhaps it was my fear of dying loveless; perhaps it was stronger than that, perhaps it was my desire to live and love fully. Perhaps it was none of these, but only a primal desperation at the possibility of throwing away the most precious of all gifts, Life. I do think that it was a combination of all these factors and more.

My mother was a formidable woman. Back in the early 40s, as a very young woman, she was the first to leave her village to travel to a distant state in search of education and vocation. Having lost her father early and being the eldest in the family, maturity and responsibility were thrust on her. She was well versed in several languages, literature, drama, religion, culture and politics. She was a free spirit who paid little heed to authority or convention. She married later than most of her peers. When my father's family sought her, she was already her own person. To this day I know her as one for whom her family is of prime importance, but whose own sense of self is of equal or greater importance—one does not come at the expense of the other.

Equally, my father was an exception to the rules of his time. He was undaunted by the woman who was suggested as his potential partner. He was proud and indifferent. When I came along (the firstborn) the centre of his universe shifted, and icon fused with idol: I became everything for him. Early, both my parents trained me to remember that I was the most important gift that they had received, and that I was a gift unto myself. More importantly, I was taught to remember that God was the towering Giver. With this sense of Giver and Gift it was also imbued in me that I was a free person who had little to fear. Such were the springs and sources of my early life.

In my late adolescent years, I began to experience the disturbance of this paradise by the surrounding culture. I began to sense that my family was losing me to the world beyond. The social guards were changing. No matter my unconventional family circumstances, convention had the last word. The world began to become a strange place for me. All life long from kindergarten to my higher degree in university, my world was female, with exclusively female friends, female teachers and other female role models and references. The only men in my immediate world were my father and my brother. This homogeneous world, along with the impartial treatment I received at home, gave me a self-consciousness based on my personhood and not my womanhood. As I completed my education this consciousness was radically shaken, and my identity took on gendered dimensions for the first time. Suddenly, I was a *woman* who *had* to be married. I was ill-prepared for this revolution that overtook me. Most of all I was puzzled at my parents' complicity in pressuring me to marry. I was puzzled at what seemed to be their betrayal of me. I did not quite understand that their own status as "proper," "responsible" parents was at stake. I remember developing an intense dislike for an uncle who loved his role as matchmaker. He was intent on getting me "settled." My life was hanging in the scales.

My world seemed to turn back on itself. Society was negating my parents' early choices for me. It felt to me as if my parents seemed suddenly to count the way in which they had reared me as inconsequential, and that I was bucking both them and the wider society, trying to remain true to the light of what I had inherited by way of love and freedom. I do remember being overcome by sheer fear, like a fly fleeing fire. The fear was made real during trips I took in my late teens and early twenties. My folks took me the length and the width of the country in search of eligible men. At first I went along, thinking that this was a wonderful way of touring India. Soon however I realised the seriousness of the mission and started to panic at being persuaded into an alliance not of my liking. I remember the priest with the outstanding pedigree, the scientist with double doctorates, the handsome naval officer with his excellent pension prospects, and all those psychiatrists (there were plenty of them for some reason!) whom I met as prospective protectors. Each one was quite willing to make his bed with me. Did they not want much out of life, I wondered? But then again, what was wrong with *me*? Why was I so strange? Why could I not comply?

I had to leave. My excuse was that I was going to pursue a higher degree. This was the only way my parents could save face among their relatives and friends. Parents have failed in their duties if they have not "settled" their children in good marriages. I owed it to them, considering all the anguish I was causing them. And so I left.

But that was then and this is now, more than twelve years later. Now I fear the future. What did I leave for? It is not altogether clear. In all sorts of ways, my life has been radically bisected by that single act of departure, marking my time before and after. I was a very young woman then, barely having stepped onto the threshold of womanhood. Among other things, I know that I was filled with a reckless optimism about life's possibilities in the realms of men and marriage. Alas, I began to see through the glass more clearly, and my illusions began to come undone. I see this best when I encounter the real lives of my Western friends caught in the vortex of romance and relationships.

Margaret, you've heard much of this before. And yet it helps to set it down like this. I, too, am at a stage when I find myself wondering about my life choices. These letters will no doubt encourage me also to think about where I have come from, where I might be going. I will try to write more in my next.

Try to stay well and think clearly. I am, of course, interested in your own ponderings on the proclivities of your culture with regards to this compulsion towards romance.

Keep writing. Stay out of trouble!

My love,
Ivy

Slipping through the Net?

England: 7th February 1989

Dear Ivy,

Many thanks for writing me so soon. I was thrilled to see your first letter waiting on the front doormat. Luckily it arrived on Saturday, so I could read it at my leisure: I made myself a cup of tea and warmed up a couple of croissants, then put my feet up to enjoy....

Ivy, thank you for taking seriously my desire—even need—to think more deeply than I ever have before about this pattern of unhealthy relationships I seem to have gotten myself into. The fact that I'm following a cultural pattern and not my own perversely inadequate way is not solace enough for me any more, and I really want to find a better response. I feel that you are one of the few friends who can really help me in this—precisely because you have the cultural detachment that none of my other friends have!

I was fascinated by your account of your own efforts to

escape your cultural fate. And yet the fear, the loss, the disorientation that such an evasion also brought in its wake. It has made me ponder my own failure—by the ripe old age of twenty-eight—to "settle down." And yet it's been my dislocation through much of my twenties—living and working in various parts of the States—that I think has spared me from some of the usual pressures to marry and "get settled." By not quite fitting—always the foreigner, the outsider—by not staying long enough in any one place, I was a little outside the normal rituals of courtship. My ambiguous status provided intelligible reasons why I was still single. For me, then, there were fewer questions about my single status, not so many attempts to matchmake (by the time people might have grown bold enough, I was away again), and fewer of the encouragements to "find a man and settle down."

But it was still there. And I have seen my friends—men and women—try to nonchalantly fend off such well-meant concern in public and yet painfully rehearse the same desires and questions to themselves in private: "What's wrong with me; why does it never work out?" It all makes one wonder: why all this pressure? Why are unsettled (i.e., unmarried) people such a threat to our societies? From what you say, this is even more the case in India than it is in the West: why this compulsive need to mate? Is it simply some evolutionary urge to keep populating the planet? Living in the States allowed me to observe the whole process with just a little more detachment, to step outside myself just enough to become aware of how many of our responses, even in an area we assume is so entirely governed by instinct, powerful emotion, passion, are in fact determined by our culture.

But you're the sociologist. Why this seemingly universal imperative to marry? Why, given the appalling statistics in the

U.S. and Europe, is the encouragement not, rather, to stay single? Not just in the sense of avoiding marriage by setting up home and entering a partnership without commitment—which seems to me solves nothing and possibly even creates more problems. But what about helping people to take seriously the possibility of satisfying lives as single people? Why is this so hard? As a single person, I know that it is hard, that our culture does not make it easy to live a fulfilled single life in community. But is this inevitable? Surely if we learned first to be content, mature adults without a mate, our choice of partner would be less likely to be driven by desperation or fear or the weight of cultural expectation.

But Ivy, I want you to tell me more: about your girlhood, your growth into womanhood, your own expectations and hopes. What led you to turn down suitor after suitor? After all, some of them sounded rather nice! And what did you make of Romance as you saw her step out of the pages of your novels, played out in real life in the States? I know that term is by now well under way, and you will be groaning under piles of marking already. But please spare an evening for your old friend! Write me another long letter!

Yours expectantly,
Margaret

Matchmaker, Matchmaker
Make Me a Match!!

Boston: February 14th, 1989

Dear Miss Margaret,

You are surely not surprised at this epistle following so closely on my receipt of your latest! It's a long, lugubrious night tonight; the rest of the world seems to be celebrating St. Valentine's Day. I'm not in the mood to follow suit, so what better way to pay tribute to the day than by responding to some of your questions in your latest letter, which arrived today?

You ask me about some of the proposals I received for marriage. You ask me what led me to turn down suitor after suitor. I have been thinking about it. Actually, I am surprising myself at my ability to be humorous as I look back. Each encounter was laced with such pathos that it finally became the impetus for my taking leave of India. Let me tell you more about the whole experience.

We complete our college education at nineteen. A year or two prior to this, parents are putting out their feelers to relatives and friends, marketing the worth of their lovely and eligible son or daughter. Especially in the case of daughters, while higher education is not held against them, it is considered best to get them married young (right after college) so that they can start their families soon. More importantly, the marriage ensures that parents' responsibilities are fulfilled. The matter concluded, all concerned can resume their lives.

So at nineteen, my parents and I started to travel to distant cities to consider marriage proposals. These proposals, the fruits of extensive familial and communal networks, meant that the two families had expressed an interest in a marriage between their children. As I have told you before, this was an interesting season in my life. I was ill prepared for the protocol and at first mostly excited and intrigued by the possibilities. It was at this time that my self-consciousness of being "strictly female" set in. Well ahead of the meeting, I was briefed on what to expect. Invariably I would be told about the good looks of the "boy," his height, his build and his complexion, his renowned family connections, his achievements by way of honours in education, his trophies in sports and art, his present income, his home ownership, his inheritance and all the special privileges that would accrue to me if I were to marry the boy. Similarly, his family would be told about my supposedly outstanding connections and appendages, about the handsome dowry that would be given, about my intellect, the fine offspring that would issue forth, and about all the other irresistible prospects a marriage to me would undoubtedly bring. I was dressed, bejeweled and schooled. My trousseau was on display. A minifeast would be prepared; the family would arrive with their son. The first scene of the first act was now set.

As you can imagine, there is much tension in the air on such occasions. Everyone is nervous and expectant, working hard to prevent any possible faux pas. The balance is precarious at this high-level meeting of diplomats. Prevarication is a much lauded art. Despite growing up in the culture, it was still an alien process to me—what was I to make of this farce of having to put out my best in order to be picked? What for? At whose expense? The dynamics of the meetings were invariably the same: the individuals would meet each other in the presence of the families; only a few pleasantries of the most innocuous nature were expected: "What is your name?" "Where were you educated?"

"What are your hobbies?" A few such questions later (nearly all initiated by the male), the two individuals were expected to report back to their respective family members. If each responded favourably, Hurrah, Ship Ahoy and Full Steam Ahead with plans for a gala celebration! If not, everyone packed up and got ready for the next show.

I was always disturbed that the exchange was so superficial. It appeared that the individuals themselves were the last consideration in the arrangement. The worst thing in my case was that all the men whom I met were agreeable to marriage with me. This was logical considering that, if the backgrounds matched, men did not have to be choosy. Any woman would do! I was the one who was looking for something more: for mutuality, for a kindred spirit, for true love. I was angry that I was not allowed to initiate or ask my own questions during that first public meeting. I was frustrated with my parents for forbidding me this privilege after a lifetime of encouraging my curiosity. I felt violated. Nobody understood. Marriage for me was a coup de grâce to the life I had led before. It all seemed so bloody cruel.

I was expected to make up my mind in a matter of hours or less and be prepared to come out with a press release explaining in sound detail why I had rejected him. After all, the family has to save face in the community. The reasons had to be serious and concrete, such as: "ugly," "limps," "violent," "lecherous," or "mentally off." Not anything "irrelevant" such as views on politics, philosophy, theology, feminism, economics or anything else. "What more do you want?" I was asked. "He is educated and drawing a five-figure salary." "She is so-and-so's daughter or niece." "He is the only son and the sole inheritor." "She is strikingly beautiful," we were told by solicitous families. My mother would ask me, "What's thirty or forty years in the larger scheme of eternity anyhow?" referring to a potentially calamitous marriage and its relative insignificance.

As a social scientist, I was equipped to understand the "rationale" behind such social institutions and practices (even as I understand the historical movement from arranged marriages to romantic attractions in Western societies). Nevertheless, I refused to become the fatted calf in the system.

Every meeting was a mixture of expectation and resignation on my part. Despite everything, I kept thinking that somehow life would work its magic in the tradition of Barbara Cartland, Denise Robbins and Hermina Black. I hoped that one of these men would dare to be different and engage my attention. And then my paradise would be restored. My family and I would both be happy. The suitor sessions in India were uneventful and unremarkable as I remember them. Yet the psychological anguish seemed interminable. I remember thinking once or twice that my will might be broken, that I would succumb and my spirit would expire. I could identify with prisoners and captives. I was close to the edge. My parents badgered me, suggesting that I would bring disrepute to the family. You see, if a daughter stays unmarried too long, she is priced out of the marriage market by virtue of her age, loss of attractiveness and success in education or employment. I realised that the best way to bring dignity to this recurring crisis was to leave. I suspect that eventually, if I had held my ground for good reason (looking after an ailing parent, sole source of income, etc.), I would have been allowed my single status. But in my day and age, in the absence of such extraneous circumstances, I would not have been spared.

My escape plan was to go away to the U.S. to do postgraduate work. As I've told you before, a few years earlier it would have been Britain, and who knows about you and me! In any case, I remember that the suitors kept coming right up to the time of my departure. My parents gave me an ultimatum. If I were to be refused an American visa (which of course was a possibility), it was a sign from God that I was meant to marry the next man. No doubt I prayed tearfully that this cup would pass. Worse, I was concerned at the dilemma before God! Who was God going to oblige and on what basis? I was alone. My life's friends were all lost to me. Occasionally when we met, we cast suspicious looks at each other. Each felt betrayed by the other. I hope you understand, Margaret, that it was not that I had rejected men and marriage for good. It was just that I needed more of a say in the procedure. As much as I had publicly disavowed the system, I always kept half an ear cocked for chance possibilities in the process. I promised my parents that I would be open to their suggestions even in the States.

Once there, these suitor setups took on bizarre turns. It was clear that the family networks were effective only up to a point. While in India one is able to make enquiries of the prospective candidate (if one so chooses) by talking to primary school teachers, old neighbours, classmates and even domestic servants; such possibilities did not exist in the U.S. Like other Westerners, these fellows led uprooted and mobile lives. They were the sole spokespersons for themselves; I had no one to do any homework on my behalf. I would have to gamble.

I have already told you some of the stories. Did I mention the case of the space scientist who flew more than two thousand miles across the States to come and see me? All signals were "go" right up to the point of his coming, and I was really quite excited. An American couple graciously took up the role of chaperones. This time, the fellow and I were to spend time alone together. At last, my chance to do it my way! We did not have a promising start. One of the first things he asked me was to guess his shoe size. This seemed a rather bizarre opening gambit and I did not know how to react. In any case, I had failed to note how unusually large his feet were. He told me. Size 14. I tried to look impressed and struggled dutifully on. After all, this was only the beginning, and this time I was determined to give it my best efforts. He had looked so good on paper!

Later on that first day, he suggested a walk by the river. On a suitable bench, we both sat down. He pulled out a portfolio from his briefcase and started to give me a lecture on the ideal Christian couple—with strong undertones about their respective sexual functions. According to this program, the husband is like a shield and spear in battle, the protector of the woman. The woman is like a vase, a receptacle of beauty and fragrance! He went on in this vein using diagrams, scripture verses and literature extensively. Harbouring serious doubts by now, I somehow managed to maintain my demure demeanour. After all, my reputation and that of my parents were at stake.

Yet, my fears continued to grow: when we were in the company of others, he appeared quite pleasant and civil; alone, he sent shivers down my spine with some of his ideas. The next day of his stay clinched it for me. While driving along, a cat crossed our path and he asked me if I liked cats. As you know, Margaret, I have no great love for cats, but keeping my parents in mind, I remained silent. What was I meant to say? He pressed me for an answer, and finding the matter of some importance to him, I gave him a vague reply to the effect of "sort of." He replied with surprising vehemence that he hated cats. In fact, he enjoyed killing them! For his scientific experiments on animals? I asked faintly. No, he insisted, he loved to kill them as a hobby. In fact he had killed over a hundred of them. I gasped. None of my careful training had prepared me for this! Would my father believe me? What if this man extended his hobby to killing wives?

Then there was the chap who flew out to meet me in the Midwest, right around the time I met you. That was also puzzling. He was a loquacious character. After excessive compliments on my culinary skills, my interests in music, my housekeeping abilities, etc., etc., and repeated assurances of calling when he got back, I never heard from him again. As you know, I was really deflated. Many months later, I heard that he got married and turned into an abusive husband. That marriage dissolved later. Then again, there was the pensive psychiatrist who even my charming New York cousin—the one you said could get a telegraph pole to talk—could not draw out. The supposed suitor sat there for an entire evening, hardly looking in my direction, let alone making any enquiries. I later discovered that he was no psychiatrist. Of course there were other more ordinary fellows—perfectly acceptable in the standard marriage stakes—along with a run of highly accomplished braggarts whose dreams for themselves were hardly mine. Such have been my suitors.

Meantime, my increasingly desperate parents continued to place matrimonial advertisements both in India and in the United States on my behalf. I remember full pages of advertisements in every national Indian Sunday newspaper. These served the urban populations who were removed from the traditional bonds of family and relations in their native villages. There were two sections: one for brides and the other for grooms. My folks ran a few. How crass the ads were! We felt like cattle on display in the Sunday market. All the "vital" information of hobbies, height, complexion, caste, class, religion, education, income, family background, schools attended and, in recent years, overseas residence and "green card" status—all these facts about us were reduced to a bland précis. Even as I was being advertised, we spent hours poring over the ads from the groom side. Somewhere in this statistical mess of bargaining and transactions, lay a mysterious human being who was known to hardly anyone, least of all to him- or herself. Hordes replied, all sorts of them—young, old, married, single, widowed, Hindu and Muslim; even those just interested in obtaining green cards would try their luck.

What was becoming of me in all of this? I was disenchanted and hopeless. I balanced this world against the world of my American friends, who were playing Russian roulette with their emotional and sexual lives, and I was filled with terror. Those early years were hard years, going back and forth in my mind about my choice to leave India, about my choice to eschew traditional marriage arrangements, about my choice to avoid Western style romance and wondering about all the promises made in the books of my youth and longing for some myself. I wondered if there would be any breakthroughs. I remember a diary entry where I pleaded with God that my need for a special relationship be taken away from me if it was not to be met.

I think that I have largely overcome the anguish and confusion of those days now, although occasionally I still feel a pang of longing for companionship. My work, my very dear friendships and my conviction that all human claims for relationships are finally spiritual quests keep me going. While I still hope for possibilities out of these suitor meetings, I am not banking on them. Life is a wonderful gift and I am determined to enjoy it—alone or in company. This is where I am at and have been for a few years now. Daily I pray that this stasis can be kept up.

It's late; I can hear some Valentine revelers wending their way home. It makes me feel somewhat wistful once again. I wish you were here to cheer me out of my melancholy. Hope all's well.

Love,
Ivy

The Romantic Imperative

England: February 25th, 1989

Dear Ivy,

Your latest letter moved me and amused me. I have often listened with fascination to your accounts of interviews with prospective husbands. I love the unexpected vistas you offer me into a whole new world of courtship with its expectations and obligations so utterly different from anything in my own experience. Do you remember the first time you regaled me with such tales? I can still recall it: me pressing for more stories, not quite able to believe that such episodes were part of the history of my closest friend, and the two of us finally collapsed in laughter, tears streaming down our faces, rocking helplessly at the absurdity of it all.

And yet, as is so often the case, maybe we laughed the harder because the underlying reality felt bleak. That's how the comedy works in Shakespeare's tragedies: it breaks the unbearable tension of unsustainable grief. But you wouldn't want me to aggrandize your episodes with such comparisons. Yet I don't think I had fully understood before how fearful you were, your real terror of being entrapped into a marriage that could so easily stifle your sense of self. Almost the image of a living tomb. Strange how your teenage friends could devour all those Mills and Boon romances and yet accept without demur a marriage arranged in such prosaic fashion, not even the least hint of romance. What made you different?

Mind you, I have never known you to be meekly happy with your lot—or, for that matter, anyone else's. You are always acutely conscious of how it should be, could be, surely must be, so much wanting to hold on to what is intensely precious to you, so conscious that it too will pass. I remember in the early days of our friendship how often I used to chastise you for your tendency to lament the passing of good times—a wonderful dinner party or a visit with a kindred spirit or a holiday—even before they had started! "Ivy's divine discontent," I used to tease you, whilst simultaneously exhilarated by your enormous zest for life, your appetite for fun, for justice…for abundance in all things. So perhaps, wherever this yearning in you came from, it was what fanned the flicker of hope in you that maybe after all it could be for you like it was in the stories.

In a way, I had no such alternatives. The Romantic Option was the only one on offer. So, the posters of pop stars, the Barbara Cartland tales, the Love Story films, these confirmed the *only* narrative of my culture. There was nothing else to aspire to. Of course we could see in the marriages of our parents and their friends that reality fell far short of the ideal. Gone, it seemed, were the passionate embraces, the red roses and champagne, the intimate gazes and melting moments. But we youngsters believed we would not betray the dream. My generation knew that we would fulfill our ideals more successfully than our parents had done. I don't think it occurred to us that there was any other ideal to aspire toward than that of falling head over heels in love and living happily, certainly passionately, ever after. The notion of "arranged marriage" would have seemed barbaric, an unforgivable violence to our individuality and freedom of choice. Yet looking back, I wonder how individual our choices really were, and how deeply we were actually choosing. The social script prescribed for us was no doubt just as limited as yours seemed to you, only we didn't realise it. Our fate was just as likely to lead to entrapment and stultification as your "arrangements," only we couldn't see the net's mesh: it was spun too fine and blended too beautifully with the dreams we thought were our own.

But I am being too pessimistic. How can I deny the undeniably wonderful aspects of romantic love? Even in my present melancholy mood, I don't believe it is all just a huge con, some massive natural confidence trick to dupe us into the demanding task of rearing children—as some deterministic scientists would have us believe. I know for myself that even despite the heartbreaks, there has been much that is deeply good in the three or four romances I have had. I can still remember the huge surge of joy when Nicky's best friend came to tell me that he wanted to "go steady" with me. He was all of twelve; I was ten, and I was deeply flattered that he had apparently given up all his other girlfriends to clear the decks for me. We had barely spoken, and although the course of our romance amounted to not a great deal more than a few pecks on the cheek before curtain up in the production of "Oliver" we were in, the pleasure at being chosen, at being found special, was very real. No doubt, as Augustine suggests, we long such ultimate longings as only God can fulfill. And the aspirations of romantic love echo aspects of that spiritual quest more than almost anything else in human experience—hence the erotic language of the Song of Solomon and the vivid love imagery of so many religious mystics.

And yet, and yet, why does it so often seem to turn to ashes in contemporary real life? Why can it begin to seem like some cruel illusion? How deeply we are written by our culture! Even as I write, I am aware that merely understanding more clearly the pitfalls does not save us from them. So, while I may *sound* mature or sussed out, the reality of my lived existence is often far from the composure I may convey. I can analyse and understand, yet, lemminglike, still feel myself irresistibly drawn towards yet another precipice.

Ivy, believe it or not, I'm trying to fend off another infatuation! I think I am developing a crush on someone I met at a party a couple of evenings ago. I'm sure nothing will come of it, and in any case, I am determined to stick to my sabbatical from men. But once again, I amaze and dismay myself at my capacity for falling for the Romantic imperative, and wonder at my vulnerability. There was a caring warmth about this man—Robin, his name was—he was intelligent and curious and gentle and, what impressed me most, he didn't seem out to impress or compete or show off. Yet, what bothers me is my seeming inability to just enjoy the fact that we spent a very pleasant hour or so talking and then let it go at that. Instead, I find myself curious about whether or not he is attached (I think not) or gay (quite possibly) or whether the attraction is mutual....I've been invited out to dinner tomorrow evening by some good friends of his. I think he might be there....But enough of this. I'm tired and am off to bed. I'll finish this tomorrow—after the dinner party.

February 27th. Oh, Ivy, Ivy. It's 3 A.M. here, 10 P.M. with you. I'd call you but I've left my address book with your phone number in my office. I need a good dose of common sense. And some hard reminders. I keep thinking about Robin. I'm infatuated and annoyed about that. It's pathetic. Why, oh why, am I so stupid and vulnerable? The dinner party last evening was wonderful—five of us—some excellent conversation, both serious and surprisingly personal, considering that it was not a group of very close friends. But somehow the chemistry worked and it felt like one of those near perfect evenings. I feel even more drawn to Robin, and I was touched by the man I saw revealed tonight…the element of pain and isolation, not to mention humour. Oh dear. And I must admit that the "Saviour of the Wounded Male" role that you have warned me about sidles to the fore. I feel that I might have so much to give him, and that I could help to end his isolation and give him the deep fulfillment that I think he longs for. Dangerous stuff, eh? And you've heard it all before. I really don't think he fancies me…although at times this evening I wondered. I think he likes me and finds me interesting, but there is also a detachment and liberality in his friendship so that I cannot take any special interest from his attention.

I really do think that we could be good friends. What worries me is the fear that all the messages about romantic love in our culture will conspire to make that impossible. He's bound to detect my attraction and be fearful that any friendliness will give me the wrong messages, whilst I, in my effort not to reveal my interest, will appear too cool and then give him the impression that I don't particularly like him and so on and so forth. I sometimes think that we as a culture seem locked into unhealthy patterns of relating, causing so much fruitless pain and damage. I'm sure that a large part of it is a longing for intimacy, more desperately sought and needed in this atomised postmodern world of ours than ever before. But are there no other ways, no other possibilities than these desperate lunges—

or temptations to lunge—into yet another relationship where we idealise the other and then want to give and receive our all?

As I grow older, I sadly watch the dreams of too many of my married friends totter and crumble, and wonder if together—as a generation, as a culture—we are being forced to try to imagine new ways of living and loving that are more in touch with reality. Must our longings be articulated, shaped, constructed and manipulated by the images of advertising, films, best-sellers? I'm not after—God forbid—some kind of prosaic, grey, lacklustre alternative, but surely there is a way of relating, of meeting and mating, that does not finally turn out to be based on fantasy, leaving our longings finally dashed? Surely there must be a way that corresponds to the deep desires of our hearts?

It seems that neither of our cultures has got it quite right. But I'm sure that each could learn something from the other. Even if it is simply the acknowledgment, the realisation that ours is not the only way, that there are alternatives to what our cultures seem to conspire to convince us is the "inevitable," the "natural." What do you think? I'd be really interested to hear your reflections on the Western concept of Romantic Love. You've had many years now to follow up on those dreams of Barbara Cartland and her crew and test them against the reality. What do you make of it all? How have you negotiated your way through this maze that is Western dating and relating? And, most pressingly for now, can you throw me a line to keep me from falling over the edge again?

Much love,
Margaret

The Dream Betrayed

Boston: March 5th, 1989

Dear Margaret,

Hearing from you by post or phone is always the high point of my day—even if it is in the cause of trying to avert another romantic tragedy! It was very good to talk with you on the phone the other night and to hear you sounding more resolved and ready to fend off capricious Cupid's latest assault. And now your recent letter has arrived.

I am often struck by the fact that no matter how engaged I am otherwise, I always find the time to be in touch. You revive me—again it is like the intimacy I knew and had as a young girl. I am amazed at how effortlessly I am able to share my life with you. I know that your childhood in Africa and your Scottishness (with reference to the English) are important dimensions to our friendship. I mean your exposure to diversity and marginality and how that relates to your understanding of my own cultural predispositions that are often markedly different from your own. No doubt the woman that you are is a composite of more than these. I am most grateful for the mutuality we share, even though externally we might appear quite different in our styles.

You tease me about my divine discontent. Indeed you are right—it is my long and often lonely conviction of the utter preciousness of life that makes me want the most for me and all the world around me. No doubt this explains my search for and relationship with God, my love for learning and teaching, for changing and for shaping—whether an idea, a sweater or bread dough. "All things bright and beautiful, all creatures great and small; all things wise and wonderful, the good Lord made them all" (remember that childhood hymn?)—surely we all want to be the means and ends of that sacred truth. Perhaps it was this deep consciousness of God's love (working out the chorus "Jesus loves me" was my earliest theological challenge in light of the colour-caste-class system I knew as a child), and God's attendant passion and desire for me (especially me and by implication all others) that kept me hungry for "more," and later even *fighting* for more as I entered womanhood. This sense of life's preciousness in the face of unremitting mortality all around us adds a great deal of urgency to our days. Is this the answer to your question—what made me long for something more?

And yet now I fear the future. You ask me what happened to all those dreams of Romantic Love inspired by my teenage readings. I brought them intact to the West and have spent time trying to match what I see with all that Cartland and Robbins wrote for me. I am almost afraid to admit what I have found here. Actually, I feel terribly betrayed by them. Perhaps I can't blame them, they were doing what they do best—writing stories for lonely people and for naive people. I should blame myself for taking them so seriously. But, how could I have known? Nobody told me the truth where I grew up. They didn't know either. I did notice that these writers were writing about romance as it appeared from the outside—the meeting, the greeting, the glamour, the perfume, the glances and dances, the embraces and kisses, the heartbreak and the chase, the flowers and the presents. I do remember that all their stories stopped at marriage or a few days thereafter. So they really did not tell me the inside out stories. Surely life is not a suspended courtship. I was left to find that out for myself. And I did. It was disheartening and frightening. I felt like those dreamers who take their dreams West to California, and disappointment drives them to perch on the Golden Gate Bridge and ponder about the meaning of it all. I wondered about God—in the East or West. God's absence was so often more keenly felt than God's presence. Loneliness and lust appear to rule in one sphere and power and pragmatism prevail in another. In some fundamental sense, all fear their mortality. All seem to long for something beyond themselves in human companionship. And I find myself stranded, trying to make sense of it all.

Soon after my arrival in the West, I began to be gripped by the same sort of panic and fear that I experienced at my possible fate in India. This fear came from somewhere deep within. It came from knowing that my options for affection and intimacy were blocked by the constraints of the culture. Let me explain more: you ask what I make of the Western game of dating and mating....

Friday nights and weekends in the States are predictable. While I am often wanting to recover from the labours of the week, most people I know are revving up for the lucky dip at the race track, firming up a courtship or looking for a new one. The effort deters hardly anyone; hope spurs them on. Most congregations of single friends have as part of their agenda therapy for their single "condition" (medicalising the issue almost), recovery from previous partnerships, or strategies for future success. Up to a point I could participate in these conversations, but soon I would think about the frequent waste of life this can be. Such endless optimism, such waiting, such desire! Sure, I empathised with these existential dilemmas of loneliness and isolation, but I often wished they could be taken to a higher order of query, of making some global connections with human alienation of other kinds, of seeing that in the end humans had no ultimate answers for other humans. I saw a parasitical existence on the part of many in these groups that tugged away at my own sense of purpose and worth.

The similarity of the quest on both sides of the world made me wonder. Had I made a mistake in avoiding marriage, in leaving India? Are all humans destined for matrimony anyway? While I have been constitutionally inclined to peer behind the veil of life's mirages by asking questions, skepticism and cynicism about the Western world of romance came about probably from knowing that my "chances" were not very good. What was I to do? If indeed I had made a mistake, should I now school myself into the art of romance? Friends told me that I would be "successful" if I made myself more "available"; one colleague was intrigued that I didn't "flirt." It was suggested that I advertise in the papers (they even ran a few ads on my behalf), and there were instances where I was "set up"—once with someone who had recently returned from the Philippines who had gone after a mail-order bride and didn't care much for the candidate. Such strategies were not only culturally alien to me, but deep down I was repulsed at all the manipulation and desperation present. The techniques seemed so artificial despite all the rhetoric of freedom and choice that surrounded me. While I was horrified at my prospects as a married woman in India, I was disappointed at my prospects as a single woman in the U.S. Some consolation was had in remembering the distance I was from India. My helplessness came from knowing how wrong both these worlds had it and wondering if any *via media* existed at all. It was frustrating to see how ill-equipped all cultures are to provide a just and due place for people to opt for the single life. It is as if the heterosexist model of existence is the only natural and virtuous state of being for virile humans.

I realised I was angry, thinking that I might have fooled myself, perhaps even angry at the world for deceiving me so. I often thought of my younger days and talked about those times with my friends who had also read those British love stories. I felt that they too had deceived me when overnight they put down the books and proceeded to say "yes" to their families and stranger-husbands. "What happened to those sweet dreams?" "Did you not kill your hopes?" These were the questions I would have loved to ask and did not dare to. I do remember a general conversation on the subject with a friend once and her reply was, "But we always knew that we were groomed to marry, no matter the books we read." I haven't quite forgotten that response. It made an impression on me. I then began to ask why I alone believed in the fantasies of romance so much. I know that I did so because of the unbearableness for me of what lay ahead for the women in my culture—early marriage and subsequent motherhood. For me then, the fantastic became more real than the real. In another sense, I suspect also that the fantasy of romance thrives in the absence of actual experience. One certainly senses that. My despair was all the greater when I came West and found what I did. Here too the individual was bereft of choice. I had to grow up fast and start discerning what it was that was important to take along for my life's journey. So that's where I am at now. Single and speculating.

As for you and men, I don't know. I grieve each time you love and lose, but each time wonder: is it this or that individual you mourn, or is it in some way related to your own interrupted dreams, abandoned possibilities? As you put it so well, you kept hoping like a compulsive gambler that it would work out on this present round. Is there any other way ahead for you? You ask for a lifeline, something to hold on to in this present infatuation. Perhaps you will enmesh yourself, but ponder this: what happens to your ideals every "next time"? Surely they are affected by the previous round. It is this phenomenon with dates and mates that frightens me about my own chances here. I am not up for it. Something doesn't seem right. Alone as I feel, I am still trying to understand "loving and losing" and the worth of it all. The anxieties are deep, the stakes are too high. While I came to the West believing in "choice" for one's life, I am struck by the absence of it. What's so different from India? Thinking about it as a Christian sheds little further light on this. I can see the workings of God's grace perhaps, but little perception of God's will in these matters. There is far too much human manipulation for God to have a fair hand. Strangely, I can see how my Indian friends might call on fate, the stars, God, etc.; but here I can hardly see even that at work.

So often we think we are free to choose. Such a prized privilege here in the West! But as one ponders on what this freedom means, one is unsettled. The highly differentiated gendered roles of males and females, the gendered images of human beauty and body, the internalisation of the "male gaze" by women and men are hugely influential in the truncated nature of choice in intimate relations. In such a weighted context, can we really talk about the exercise of free will? I think perhaps Voltaire got it wrong in thinking that people are born free but are found everywhere in chains. I rather think that we are born into the fetters of culture and perhaps die free. What do you say?

Margaret, for all the pressures that you are under—recovery from Brad and now this present crush especially—I can, at the risk of sounding glib, only promise to pray for God's grace as you ride this one out. It is not easy. It can't be easy—this prayer for patience, for clarity, for self-surrender, for obedience and most of all for this mysterious grace we trust in for blessedness through and beyond all of this. Margaret this is another long one.

So long and much love,
Ivy

The Romantic Comedy

England: March 20th, 1989

Dear Ivy,

Many thanks for your phone call and your letter. The immediate danger is over—or at least feels a little less acute. I'm not about to fling myself into the arms of an eagerly waiting Robin and be swept off with him into the melting sunset. Your last letter was really helpful. Already, in the cold light of day immediately after posting my last letter to you, I felt somewhat more composed about Robin. I wasn't even sure about sending you that letter—so full of teenage-style impulses and irrationalities and second-rate preoccupations. But you're my best friend. I'm grateful you take me as I am and understand my weak spots whilst not simply indulging them.

During the last few weeks, I have managed to do some thinking for myself and have managed to arrive at some sort of more ordered emotional state. God knows, there is room in our world for extremes of feeling and passion, but too easily such emotions seem self-absorbed and destructive—to ourselves as well as to others. Why do I waste so much of my energy and passion on such fruitless infatuations? It's not as if there is any want of far more worthy causes to sigh and cry for. This regular dissipation of my energy frustrates me!

Nevertheless, I have not yet got beyond this pattern, have not yet graduated to a more focused way of living and loving, so, dear friend, please bear with me. Last weekend I took a group of visiting American students up to Edinburgh as part of their British Culture tour. It was really good to get away! I like working here, but it can feel like a very small world sometimes, and, in the slightly hothouse atmosphere that prevails, I'm sure emotions grow faster and relationships become more intense than are normal. Getting out of it for four days was refreshing and, in some ways, sobering. One of the American students has a big crush on one of the lads in the group. It was rather obvious, and I kept wishing that she wouldn't make it quite so evident, that she wouldn't appear so available for him and would maintain more distance and dignity. Love, however, is not always a very dignified affair. The young woman is by no means immature, and watching her was quite a warning for me: I'm keen to play it cool as far as Robin is concerned. I really doubt that he's interested—he's made no attempt to get in touch—and I don't want to embarrass him and me by being overattentive or unnatural when next we meet.

The other slightly sobering realisation for me came on the first night of our trip away. Jamie, one of my friends in Edinburgh, had arranged a party for us in his flat, to give the American students a chance to meet some local people and experience some Scottish hospitality. One of his friends was a rather charming young minister named Malcolm who rounded off the evening with a brilliant recitation of *Tam O'Shanter*, the long poem by the great Scots bard, Robert Burns. Ivy, with your penchant for poetry and recitation, you would have been in your element. What concerned me just a little was the way I felt drawn to this chap and how pleased I was when he suggested that we meet up again—along with Jamie—the next morning for coffee. I was excited and yet bothered again at the evidence of my own "flakiness," as the Americans call it—the sort of emotional unreliability that seems endemic to the single state of the young Westerner. Here I am fending off an infatuation with one man and within weeks, find myself attracted to someone else as well.

The coffee meeting was, I must confess, very enjoyable. I found Malcolm to be intelligent, amusing and apparently with a number of interests and perspectives that appear close to my own. Yet one of the most attractive aspects about him is, for me, his Scottishness. I was drawn to his accent, his red hair and pale, freckled complexion, his classic Scottish tweedy dress style, "exquisite in its own genre" as I explained to my amused codriver. I probably won't see this chap again—although he did invite me most warmly to look him up next time I'm in Edinburgh. But it's interesting how much more important it is to me now than it used to be to find someone from my own culture. Maybe it's part of the growing realisation that partnerships are about so much more than the two individuals concerned, that marriages are of communities as well as individuals—something that your tradition takes altogether much more (too?) seriously. Maybe, after my various cultural shifts, I feel the need for some cultural integration in my life and find myself almost automatically interested in a man who offers to provide it. At any rate, the little heart flutter in Edinburgh was helpful in contextualising here: at least when one's interests are divided, it's harder to take any one too seriously. And impossible to cast oneself as the tragic romantic heroine! Oh fickle romance!

So, despite my enjoyment of the quickening pulse and the suspense and the boost to the confidence that comes with being found attractive, I am also a little saddened again at my emotional vulnerability. It makes it all the clearer to me that it is as much my own needs and longings that dictate the pattern and focus of my infatuations as the men themselves. The romantic imperative again. I must confess that I enjoy some appreciative male attention, but it worries me to think that my "sparkle" depends on it, that my vivacity, my joie de vivre might rely, to some extent, on this pattern of infatuation which—whether in long or short cycles—seems to colour the pattern of my life.

And so I continue to wrestle. I am grateful at least for this weekend's delightful—but informative—perspective on the Romantic Comedy, and shall not be offended in the slightest if you indulge in a gentle chuckle at my expense. Look forward to hearing from you.

Love,
Margaret

Towards Liberation

Boston: April 5th, 1989

Dear Margaret:

Lovely to hear from you again. I must say that I am endlessly fascinated by your days across the Atlantic, more intrigued really. Now that you are on home ground the floodgates of your psyche and soma appear to have given in, and you are like a child mesmerized by the thrill of naughty play in the fountain spray on a hot summer day. Yes, on the face of it, your report on Robin and Malcolm appear as passing infatuations and thus comic, but you also seem to be recognising the seriousness of what in fact might be going on, and here probably lies your own deliverance. Amidst all the energy these flights of fancy sap from you, you also write of shared values, your desire to make a difference in someone's life, your own search for roots and your perception that relationships are communal also. These are important issues to wrestle with. Don't be too hard on yourself. As long as you stay away from life-binding choices, remember that the present phase you are in is all too "normal." After all, you are home, no longer a visitor or a guest. The world around you rightfully makes its demands on you. Finishing a Ph.D. or some other project is no longer a pressing preoccupation. "You *must* match and hatch" is the coded subtext you are receiving from friends and family. This then becomes your next project to accomplish. Few humans can stand the risk of remaining truly individual. There are no cultural supports for such a stance. Against such a social context it will not be easy for any of us to plot an alternative path.

Beyond the dictates of one's culture, I am struck by recent

reports in medicine and anthropology that state that attractions, affairs, sexual behaviour and other intimate interactions are also governed by genes, hormones and other physiological factors. While I do not want to settle for such determinism, they serve to highlight some of the complexities of what we humans are up against. I can see how cultures might comply with and subvert such biological tendencies in order to make societies more viable for systematic and organised propagation.

Ah, Margaret, writing to you is becoming a heart- and head-warming exercise for me, especially as I am compelled to put on paper those aspects of my life that I have come to take for granted, those aspects that are too precious, too private, too painful to recall and still too present. One is frequently so consumed by the affairs of the day that one forgets to remember one's own remarkable journey. At least I do. In any case what good does it do to remember in a world so far from my own roots, so alien to my heritage, a world in which the core of me is more enigmatic than accessible, so alone really?

You might wonder how I respond to these cultural dictates. What shall I say? I am not sure that there are turning points in one's life, except when one is living in some sort of a war zone. Yes, there are persons, events, decisions, etc.; but I believe that these occur/exist largely in the context of continuity. I have written to you before about the enormous inheritance I received from my parents, but insofar as turning points go, I know that my departure from India was critical. In a rather Frostian sense I did choose the road less taken. The rest of my journey has been radically shaped by that unnerving and threatening decision to leave home, to leave the comforts and certainties of convention and risk the flight of freedom in more ways than I can fully comprehend now or in the future.

Thinking about what it takes for an individual to take a critical and independent stance, the lesson I have learnt in my life retrospectively is that individuals break loose when their very lives are under threat. Some take their own lives (as I have known), others leave (such as myself), others disengage from the culture at great cost (as some of my friends have), retreating to religion, depression, child rearing and so on. In any case, immediate or imminent threats to one's life often lead to the alteration of the journey. Clearly, I did not know the implications of my trajectory ahead (one hardly ever does). But as a result of my resistance, life became exceedingly precious, and that knowledge dictates my life in the West. I think of that memorable line in the film *My Brilliant Career* where the protagonist (I forget her name) says, "Loneliness is a terrible price to pay for independence." On the one hand she is so right, yet if one has a sense that one's life has been graced by God, I am not sure that loneliness is an inevitable price. If one chooses independence because one values life and loves life, then it seems to me that that conviction is sufficient in itself.

Yet a mere cognitive understanding of one's raison d'être is not enough for such liberation. I think that the statement is also a social commentary on the predicaments that many women find themselves in uniquely. For so long seen as a mere male appendage, the society and she are little equipped to take her on her own terms. Even your letters attest to that. The fact is that while I have lived for more than twelve years as a single woman, I had to leave India to be able to do so. Culture always demands loyalty from those it claims as its own. This is illustrated by your statement in one of your earlier letters that the expectations of you as a single woman were held in abeyance somewhat when you were in the

States. Your friends and colleagues here viewed you as a sojourner, with sufficient unknowns about you—British, visiting, possible boyfriend back home, etc. This has been even more the case with me, as I am viewed clearly as a resident alien—Eastern, bonded to family, inclined to marry strangers, or betrothed at birth and so on. I have been told so by many friends. And then there have been the few provincial chauvinists who proceed to ask if I am in a "relationship," if I am "seeing" or "going with" someone, or if they can help "set me up." Overall I have been able to utilise the chasms in convention to my advantage by freeing myself from the pressure to find and keep someone. For me to contemplate a relationship here in the West is as preposterous as it was to consider a marriage in India. Somehow the circumstances seem contrived in both cases. Yet—and yet—I still have to address my aloneness. My reference groups in both my worlds (in India and in the U.S.) are clearly centering their lives around marriage and maternity or paternity as the case may be. The letters that I get from India inform me of marriage and motherhood **and**...what am I thinking??? In my weaker moments, I question the wisdom of my choice. But then I pick myself up, remembering that in a sense I had no choice.

I am aware that your circumstances and choices are markedly different from my own, but at some deeper level I do think that they are not all that alien. After all, both of us are barraged by the limitations of our respective worlds and our selves. I find my help in the possibility of a God who delights in wholeness and justice for humanity—individuals and groups, and for the earth at large. As usual this is getting long. Write soon. I look forward to your next. Don't forget to turn your eyes to the Cathedral towers and your ears to its bells once in a while and put your short life in perspective.

My love,
Ivy

INTERLUDE

As I reread these letters, now with the perspective of some years distance, I am struck again at the amount of energy our single status demanded from each of us. For Ivy, there was the constant awareness that she was living at odds with two cultures: she had rejected the Indian way of marriage as it had been presented to her as a young woman, and yet she was disillusioned with the reality of Romance as it was played out in the Western culture in which she had now made her home. For me, there was the usual pattern, known all too well by those in the West whose first romance does not turn out to be the final one, of the emotional roller-coaster of falling in and out of love. At times, I may seem rather bleak in my indictment of it. And I would not want to ignore its allure or the immense joy of being in love. Perhaps what comes out in these letters is something of the weariness, the sense that the pattern is repeated with little to show for it. One's own heart—and the hearts of others—gets battered, and perhaps more frustratingly for me than the pain of all this was the sense that there were so many other important things to which I wanted to give my wholehearted attention. I wanted somehow to have the matter settled, to know that I would be single for life and learn to enjoy the benefits of celibacy, or to find a partner and, together, get on with a life bigger than the sometimes narcissistic preoccupations of Romantic Love.

And yet, it never seemed so simple. So, for Ivy, suitors would still come, parents and family would still have to be answered, and her aloneness and sense of isolation in the West—despite many dear friends—would still leave a void that posed questions with the sharpness of a pain that demanded answers. For me, relating to men seemed to grow more complex as I approached my thirties. I was reaching a stage when single men of my age were perhaps, like me, growing impatient to settle down, and intimate friendship with married men no longer seemed so simple. How does one cope with such a limbo?

The letters to Ivy, along with our phone conversations, were a crucial strand in trying to go beyond the helpless pattern of simply trying to keep one's head above water whilst being buffeted by the waves of one's own emotions as well as all the various cultural influences and expectations. In the course of writing these letters, it became more possible to disentangle some of these motives and influences and, with greater distance, the way opened up for greater reflection. In various ways, people find different opportunities for such reflection: journals, therapists or simply talking with good friends. Once again, the fact that Ivy was Indian was, for me, crucial. Catching glimpses into how such matters were negotiated in a different culture, having someone who understood so well the machinations of two contrasting cultures, offered me an unusual and invaluable vantage point from which to try and work towards something more constructive, more hopeful.

So, still on rough terrain and facing new challenges and adventures, the pilgrims' progress continues. But with the sense, now, that it **is** a progress, that a track has been discerned that moves on from the muddy, much trodden ground of circuitous Romantic Love and Arranged Marriage to something approaching more solid ground—not verdant pastures, to be sure, but at least a track which holds out the promise that it might sustain the weight of our hopes.

PART TWO

The Road Less Traveled

Being Alone

England: April 11th, 1989

Dear Ivy,

Your last letter made me think a lot. I'm grateful for your understanding of what feels to me like my emotional irresponsibility. Yet you refuse to simply indulge it. Once again, you offer me more of a context in which to understand myself within my culture and remind me of the wider narrative of faith that is the backdrop, no, the very bedrock, of all our aspirations. Greater understanding nearly always leads to greater freedom; this scrutiny of Romantic Love that has been the main topic of our recent letters, has been immensely helpful in prising my emotional structure free from the heart of its illusive grip. My move, with your help, to a space just slightly closer to the margins of my culture has offered an invaluable vantage point from which to view the tragicomedy of Romance with just sufficient distance to protect me from being swept once again into its maelstrom. At least for a time.

The infatuation with Robin seems to have run its course. Not much to feed it as our paths don't really cross that much. I am feeling more settled, less emotionally adrift, and I am developing a wider circle of friends here that offers more of the kind of intimacy that is nourishing without being complicated or destructive. In particular, I have been getting to know a very interesting man here (safely and very happily married), Joel Frens, who is over from the States on research leave for six months, with a study in the department. He's working on post-colonial theory, so I may get him to contribute to one of my special topics seminars in due course. His wife, Barbara (or Barb, as he calls her), had to stay in the States with their teenage children: a bad time for their schooling to be disrupted. I think she plans to visit soon, so I hope to meet her then. Anyway, Joel and I have developed a very easy rapport, he's typically American: open and friendly and very easy to get to know quickly. We share so many of the same intellectual interests. And he is also a man of faith. I think he is as grateful as I am to have someone with whom to discuss all manner of things.

So, life here is beginning to settle down into a rhythm, and the taking stock I set out to do at the beginning of this correspondence, while far from finished, can assume a more reflective pace. It doesn't feel so driven by the hurricanes of emotional turbulence. As the matters of term wind down, I am grateful to have more time alone and more opportunity to gather myself and try to think in ways beyond simply reacting to the crisis of the moment. What you said about your own experience of loosening yourself from the path laid down by your culture in order to try to find an alternative path struck many chords in me. Although our journeys are different, I see you as someone who is further along the kind of road—independent, questioning, questing—that I would also like to be on. I was encouraged by the comforting thought that although it can sometimes feel lonely, this is not the inevitable price of independence, of striving after a more excellent way.

I am slowly learning to be alone. It is not always easy, yet I become more and more convinced that this is a part of authentic adult life—maybe even a necessary precondition. As you know, I am the gregarious sort and often my first instincts are to seek out friends in times of crisis or of joy. And that is often good. But for me it can also be a kind of evasion. I am seeking reassurance or comfort or distraction when what I sometimes need is the opposite: not to be shored up on the battered remnants of my cultural imperatives, but to let the chill wind blow around and through them, probing their fragility. From this kind of doubt, even desperation, comes, as you said in your last letter, the flight for freedom.

I am also trying to be more faithful in prayer. Everyone who tries this knows how hard it is, how everything conspires to distract one: the compassionate phone call, the ironing, the letter too long unanswered, or even the need for just that little bit longer in bed. And yet as I struggle to resist these temptations to avoid prayer, I increasingly see them as yet more conspiracies to enmesh us in the relentless treadmill of unreflective living. I have a very dear friend who lives nearby; she believes it is her vocation to live a life of contemplation in the midst of a very ordinary life. I have been astonished at how much this seems to unsettle her fellow Christians. In the face of her attempts to divest herself of the usual business, the round of superfluous obligation that constitutes so much of our lives, they scurry around trying to organise her to be energetic in a whole plethora of worthy causes. Although I know that her path often seems lonely and is not always easy, I am deeply grateful for the reminder that she is—to me, at least, but no doubt to others too—an alternative to living unquestioningly by the compulsions of our culture. It's not surprising that many find her way deeply disconcerting or even utterly incomprehensible, but in such a witness, I believe, are the roots of something quite radical.

For me at present, my own quest is still far from anything so alternative. Yet in the gradual gathering of focus in my life, there is discernible change. It seems that with each reaching into the silence, more energy is liberated for concern for others. With roots more firmly established in God—and not merely feebly grasping the rubble on the surface—there is more freedom for creative service. And as I learn more about the lives of some of those who are doing most to work for peace and justice on this earth, I am impressed and intrigued to see how their lives are so often grounded in contemplation, in prayer, in seeming inaction. I used to think, Martha-like, that "spirituality" and long periods of aloneness and prayer were a touch self-indulgent. And no doubt they can be. But increasingly, I discover how hard this path can be! It is my indulgent self that clamours and protests when it sees me preparing to sit down to pray and reflect.

So, Ivy, no impending cliffs for you to rescue me from, no knights in shining armour for you to head off: just a slightly melancholy but more peaceful friend who is learning the acceptance—and even the joys—beyond the anguish of being alone. But she still appreciates letters. Write soon.

Much love,
M.

Surrendering Our Idols

Boston: April 21st, 1989

Dear Margaret:

It was really, really good to get your recent letter. The task of deconstructing and decentering can be immensely liberating, especially in one's personal life. Faith can be foundational to this exercise, and it appears that you might be glimpsing the blossoms of this effort. Prayer for grace is crucial as we wade through the murky waters of our lives.

The more I think about what beleaguers us as young women, the more I see that in significant ways we are the culture and the culture is us. Our faith starts us on a different journey, one of redemption (from these cultural traps presumably), which we will not complete in this life. To seek wholeness and freedom we need to understand the names and the natures of demons we are possessed by, and then we can start the exorcism, the dispossession. I am of course talking about the idolatry of our selves as being the centre of all existence, of our sexuality as central to our human identity, of our acquisition of "relation-ships," all the "ours" that we so dearly live for and by. We must become idoloclasts of these.

In so many of our letters we have been very good at cultural criticism, but as religious women we know also that in the end the "enemy's last outpost is in one's own head." So there is a sense in which we need to take a frontal view of ourselves, our own corruptibility, to be able to see the lie in our souls. A disposition towards God helps us here.

As one who draws on the Christian tradition while pondering on evil, I often ask why this must be so. Is God so mean-spirited? If not, then why are these idols put in our way? Perhaps I ask the wrong questions. You and I are both well aware of the complexities of social realities—how much we participate in their coming about...the self-indulgence, the disrespect for values and institutions, the consequent social and spiritual breakdown—including the realms of intimacy, celibacy, sexuality, etc. So in one sense, it is irrelevant to talk of God in this context of our construction. God begins to take on significance when we consider the falseness of the idols we chase. We become idoloclasts as we draw near to God, when we discover the truth of the Sanskrit, "Neti, neti"—meaning "not this, not that." The Bible says something similar in the books of the Psalms and the Prophets. It is not at all surprising that God is absent in the gods of this world, "God alone is," and this is the lesson we learn as we pursue our smaller gods. I suspect that we hurt so badly because we are looking for the ultimate in the intermediate. Yet the two are not so divorced, the transcendent rests in the immanent, the grace of God has to do with our finding God's possibilities for us in the "intermediate." For you and for me, this involves finding God's possibilities as we wrestle with our humanity in the midst of our singleness, our infatuations, our sexual energies, our longings to get it right. Faith is a necessary starting point for me. I see no other way of approaching the mystery of the "here and now," the "there and shall be."

It may very well be that I take the approach I do because of my present location. The cultural constraints on me allow me the capacity to dissect and *consider* what I see. In your case, you are being remarkably "normal" in a cultural sense, even though you come up against roadblocks in the process. Deep down you know that infatuation, attraction, falling in love are all common habits in the love cycle one cultivates in the West. The songs, the music, the media, the recreations, the entire society point to the desirability, the normality and the necessity of the procedure of the heterosexist motif of intimacy. Since there are no other alternatives, you work mighty hard at getting this right. I, on the other hand, for many of the reasons mentioned in previous letters, have my hands and heart tied to a great extent. In such a position I am compelled not only to compare and contrast cultures, but I am also forced to wonder about God in all this. I too am forced to come to terms with my deep aloneness, with my future. This aloneness is compounded by my self-knowledge as one who is in exile not merely geographically but more importantly culturally, saying no to all the yeses that surround me.

What I find most disturbing about Western culture is its rather narrow conception of intimacy, often reducing it to the sexual in some form or other. Only the other day I saw a big tin of Danish butter cookies in the shop, and all around and over the tin were the cherubic representations of a little boy and girl walking hand in hand, on a swing together, etc., etc., clearly relating to one another romantically. No doubt some must have found it "cute." I looked at it and sighed, thinking—what hope for another imagination?

It is also the apparent near absence of social (cultural) restrictions governing such intimate relations that forebodes ill for the social fabric of any society. No doubt you see me coming from my own rather restrictive background, but I do wonder if cultures should indeed perform a "service" function in terms of preserving and protecting the well-being of their people through the exercise of some restrictions and regulations (I am not talking about some totalitarian state here). Certainly, one finds this happening in traditional societies but increasingly less so in modernising societies. It would be nice to envisage the transformation of the idea of individual freedom from the context of libertine understandings that prevail now.

The culture of romance introduces habits and practices that seem to be spontaneously woven into one's sociality. So it is not uncommon for men and women to be befriending each other as strangers in public places such as airports and restaurants. I for one am nervous about how to handle such situations, having been brought up in a culture where you did not speak to people you did not already know (certainly not between the sexes). I do think such free relations between people have their ramifications. I remember an essay in a book by James Luther Adams that quoted a social scientist as having stated that in our present day all adults are in a special way "permanently available" as potential marriage partners, whatever their current age or marital status. This is a frightening possibility, and yet perfectly understandable given the prevailing cultural proclivities. Any consideration of an alternative ethic for sustainable human relationships cannot avoid these enormous predilections in one's culture.

I wonder what God has in store for me? I too want to get it

right for all our sakes. So my thoughts don't come from any great wisdom on my part; rather, they arise out of my isolation and ponderings of the true nature of joy and freedom.

Margaret, it is very good that you have that contemplative friend near by. I hope she can be an encouragement. I pray that you stay the road you are on.

Love,
Ivy

The Celibate Challenge

England: April 28th, 1989

Dear Ivy,

Thank you again for a thoughtful letter. Your comments about our human tendency towards idolatry—especially in our quest for human love and intimacy—reminded me of some of the insights in D. H. Lawrence novels. During my Ph.D. work on him, I came to see that he is not so much the steamy prophet of sex, as popular report would have him. More than any other writer I know, Lawrence explores and exposes the way in which the attempt to place too much meaning on the sexual relationship is doomed to failure. Another human being cannot take the place of God; neither can the sexual relationship, however promising or absorbing, supply a complete social and spiritual context. This *egotism à deux*, as Lawrence calls it, this kind of self-sufficient, all-absorbing relationship between a man and a woman, in which every emotional need would be met, is shown time and time again in his novels to be impossible to sustain and, if pursued, deathly. Yet he also captures in his characters more deeply, more achingly, more accurately than any other writer I know, the powerful, almost religious yearning for just such all-encompassing human love. Humans do indeed seem to need some sort of absolute, ultimate kind of love; and yet, we ourselves are incapable of absolutely loving in this way.

Of course, Lawrence does not go on to give a Christian answer to this conundrum. Far from it! Indeed, he blames the Christian heritage for getting us Westerners into the mess we are in about sex in the first place! Be that as it may, I continue to agree with you when you say that perhaps it is only some kind of faith that can start us on a different journey of redemption, that can begin the process of liberation. Grace. To accept the limitations of our humanness and our need to connect but not assume that our searching can only be answered in sexual part-nership or intimacy. What we really yearn for is something much bigger and more expansive than what one other per-son—however wonderful—can give us. And yet it is this truth that our respective cultures, in different ways, seem to conspire to keep from us. Your culture seems to insist on identity and significance through marriage and family; mine offers the lure of personal fulfillment through romantic love. Neither prospect is true.

I heard a Roman Catholic priest give a talk on celibacy last week and found it extremely helpful. I suppose, like many of my culture and generation, I tend to think of celibacy as the absten-tion from sex. Of course, it means much more than this. He described how it bears witness to one aspect of the love of God. It is the relinquishing of love for a particular partner in order to be free to love everyone. I was struck by the similarities in what my contemplative friend Amy is attempting: this divestment of some of the norms of our common life—not because they are bad—but as a witness to something else, to a reality that lies beyond this. Am I making sense? The whole notion of celibacy has grasped me deeply, but I don't find it easy to explain without sounding airy fairy or spiritually pretentious. It involves a deliberate decision to live in a certain way—even when it is one's circumstances that seem to determine that decision (no one to marry, etc.). It's about embracing a particular perspective, opting to try to live by a certain untrammeled attitude.

This is far from easy for most Westerners. Life in Western societies has become so incredibly complicated in the last few decades. I am amazed when I hear about my mother's girlhood in a peasant family in the Highlands of Scotland and realise how very different it was from my own and how different mine is from my small nephew's. Living in touch with the pulse of life and God and nature is fraught with obstacles. It is not that I want to idealise the old days. Even as I am nostalgic for the intimate and innocent sense of community that my mother could take for granted as a girl, I am also appalled at much of the sheer drudgery of my grandmother's life. Of course, she probably didn't see it like that at all; I'm projecting back the horror of a late twentieth-century life that has been schooled to find its significance in things other than the unremitting rhythm of milking cows, feeding hens, cooking, cleaning, washing, child rearing and other tasks in the never-ending toil of staying alive in pre-industrial society. And yet some of that self-evidently useful rhythm is also deeply attractive to many of my generation. The freedom that technology has brought is both a blessing and a curse. The new opportunities, the plethora of choices bring both liberation, but also the possibility of just another kind of treadmill.

As I see it, the celibate calling is one that tries to stand back from the natural cycle of apparently self-justifying generation (of "birth, copulation and death" as T. S. Eliot wearily refers to it in one of his poems), whether of children or of repeating cultural expectations. I am not convinced that I am called to be celibate—or at least to live without a partner—for the rest of my life, but I find the challenges and claims that such a lifestyle makes really worth wrestling with. It represents a deeply attractive option for me right now. I think one of my fears previously had been the prospect of living without sex. Contemporary commercial culture tells us that such a denial is unthinkable. And yet, I've managed for the past twenty-eight years without too much sense of deprivation! (In any case, I think that for most people—certainly most women—it is not so much the sex that they really crave, but the warmth of intimacy that human touch can represent.) The celibate vocation reminds us that our ultimate yearning is for God. "My heart is restless till it finds its rest in thee," as St. Augustine, that oh so reluctant celibate, said all those years ago.

Certainly, whatever my future holds by way of human partnership, I need to take this deeply to heart. Again, I am reminded of D. H. Lawrence. Toward the end of his life, he wrote of human beings having two sets of desires: one superficial and immediate, the other much deeper and hidden. He describes how easy it is to be aware of the superficial desires: they are constantly clamouring for our attention, demanding prompt action, speedy satisfaction. Yet attending to these desires so easily obscures that deeper vein of longing in us, the yearning for more lasting satisfaction, for faithfulness, chastity, for the love that is found only in God. I think that the vocation to celibacy is rather like refusing to satisfy our immediate cravings for satisfactions—even if they appear to be legitimate longings for human love or success. It calls us to pause, to listen and to take heed of those deeper promptings of the spirit that reveal to us a whole set of desires more profound than we can even properly articulate. It is these desires that lead us to prayer and by God's grace, to Love.

Enough thinking and reflecting. Life, of course, goes on in its daily pattern, and I wouldn't want to pretend that I am being more of a hermit than I really am! I had a wonderful evening at the Frenses' the other night. Joel's wife, Barb, is over for a couple of weeks' holiday, and they had a small dinner party for some of Joel's new friends here. It was one of those memorable evenings when the company is relaxed, conversation is by turns hilarious and absorbing...and the wine flowed freely. It turns out that Joel is a superb cook. He decided to try his hand at something typically English for Barb's benefit, so we had roast lamb in an exquisite sauce. I don't suppose they ate lamb in the Garden of Eden, but if they did, I can now imagine such a meal with all the intensity of its first bursting unsullied upon palates undulled by mediocrity. "Ah, so this is what lamb tastes like!" No wonder the French take their food so seriously. It, too, has revelatory properties!

Barb seems very nice and I don't think was too overwhelmed at suddenly entering this new world that her husband has come to know quite well. This is the first time in their marriage that they have been apart for more than a few days, so it must all be a bit strange for them. Theirs seems a close marriage and despite having been together for some two decades (Americans do marry so very young!), they still seem to enjoy each other hugely. I just hope the rest of us did enough to make her feel included in all the conversation: she's not an academic and, unlike Joel, she's a little shy. But she seemed to be enjoying it all as much as the rest of us.

So much for my abstemious life: and yet the hilarity and splendour of that evening (like so many of the dinner parties you and I have enjoyed together) is all a part of a kind of celibacy that points to ultimate realities. I often think such evenings, with their warm company and wonderful feasting, are like a foretaste of heaven. It's captured in your comment last time, the transcendent resting in the immanent and finding God in the intermediate. Our downfall comes when we mistake icon for idol and stop short of what and Who it is we really seek.

But I'm getting philosophical again. I'd better stop here. This comes with my warmest love as usual.

Take care,
M.

Celibacy Integrated

Boston: May 7th, 1989

Dear Margaret,

Thank you for your good letter. Our letters seem to be more like a literary conversation, where each picks up on the other's previous comment or question. I certainly don't seem to be telling you about the mundane here. I am more interested in the palpable learning that takes place through our letters. It is not right to divorce philosophy from reality. I remember Foucault, the French social philosopher, saying that an idea or thought is itself an act. Certainly, we are all sums of myriads of ideas and opinions that have been translated for us through the various institutions of our lives, including our letters!

There are a few points you make in your letter that set me thinking. I would love to pursue them just a little bit more here. Throughout our correspondences, we have implied that our sometimes manic search for intimacy in a sexual context is deep down, a search for God. I have been wondering about this. It may well be the case, since we don't seem to be quite so obsessed with our quests for food or fresh air except in the event that we are dis-eased. Yet, as I think further about this search for sexual intimacy as an underlying search for God, I am not quite so convinced. The idea does not take into account sufficiently the real elements of power, conquest and self-aggrandisement that are at work in *all* people, theist and atheist alike. Each of us is in varying degrees combinations of the noble and the ignoble, the sacred and the profane, and we do well to be cognisant of this potential in us. We are by now familiar with food addictions and sex addictions, which have very little to do with food or sex.

I was very interested in your discussion of celibacy. For me the dictionary meaning of "celibate" as one who is unmarried or bound not to marry (implying sexually inactive), falls short both philosophically and culturally. Celibacy is not an adjunct existence; it is part and parcel of living married or unmarried. I agree with you that celibacy is about so much more than—and about something quite distinct from—merely abstaining from sex. Celibacy takes on significant meaning when it is a choice for a greater love than the love of self or some particular "other."

Gandhian philosophy is remarkable in placing celibacy on an altogether different plane. Gandhi's writings and his life show him weaving celibacy *into* the married state (no different from fasting and other forms of restraint). Celibacy in marriage would mean a period of sexual retreat, no different than when the spouses forsake food while fasting or undertake some other penance for the sake of physical, mental and spiritual purification. Always, such pursuits are undertaken with some higher goal in mind—to rescind the chains of desire and want that make up human bondage. It is not unlike your surrender of chocolate during Lent! Such practice is significant to show that humans do not have the last hold over their lives—nothing is that supremely important. As far as conjugal sexual relations is concerned, the commitment to celibacy comes about through joint consideration. It is not an arbitrary decision; neither is it a decision to return to the unmarried state permanently. It is merely a temporary suspension of sexual activity for spiritual reasons. Of course this is problematic for those who perceive sexual intercourse as central to conjugal health. Gandhi suggests (and I can see his point) that periodic sexual restraint is equally important for the bloom of the marriage relationship.

Celibacy, when undergirded by choice, is an all-expansive

state of being for all of us, in or out of marriage. It seems to me that Gandhian thought, rather than being a contradiction, is an extension of other religious discussions on the matter. I think that the implications of this understanding are quite far reaching. I can't help but thinking that somewhere in this perspective lies the recognition first of "Absence" and then the subsequent search for more: for "Presence," as Martin Marty has written. It is in his book, *A Cry of Absence*, (the one I gave you a couple of birthdays ago) that he writes, "Even the hedonist....thinks *some* second order of thoughts during the boredom and sadness that can follow the thrill of sexual intercourse. Somewhere there must be connections, clues, plots" (p.14). Presumably, your contemplative friend Amy has some sense of this.

Yet it seems that we cannot understand sex and celibacy without taking the discussion further. Both exist in the further understanding of Eros. This again is an easily misconstrued word. Far from being reduced to the category of the carnal, in its broadest sense it encapsulates all creative energies bestowed to humans. Baking bread, ironing clothes, housecleaning, playing the flute, writing poetry (even letters!), woodworking, painting, teaching and all those things that bring joy and facilitate connections are expressions of Eros. At least this is what I am learning these days. I find this understanding immensely empowering for all of us—that creatures and creation continue outside the male-female *sexual* fold. One might dare say that Jesus' life exemplifies the culmination of Eros in his highly energised passion for God and the world. His example remains a daunting challenge.

What we make of intimacy and human friendship is yet another discussion to have. I am struck by the absence of intimate friendships that encourage and nourish people. Somehow it appears that our lifestyles don't allow for serious and sustained friendships. All the more, the pressure is on to find the one significant relationship and be done with all others. I do sense a hidden compulsion towards relationships with the opposite sex. Somehow, those relationships are primary for the completion of one's social status. In my own life here, while I am naturally drawn to single women for no other reason than that they are free of encumbrances, they are hard to come by. And when I do, I find them preoccupied with their search for their "other." I give up and associate with older married couples. This makes our friendship—yours and mine—all the more gratifying. What are your thoughts M? Let me know. I must sign off now.

Love,
Ivy

Dangerous Liaisons?

England: May 12th, 1989

Dear Ivy,

It was so good to talk with you on the phone last night. Joel's revelation is still with me. Today, the feelings of confusion are more diffuse and unsettling. The implications of Joel's words are gradually sinking in. At one level, it was very innocent. He really is a good, pure man, and I still do believe that his marriage is essentially sound. The way he talks about his wife and clearly misses her, his delight in her and love for her, I know that none of that is qualified by his conversation with me yesterday in my office.

So why did it disturb me so much? I keep going over our brief meeting in my mind. As I told you, we were talking in my office after departmental coffee about a class we are working on together. Just as we were wrapping up, he said he wanted to apologise for all the stuff he's been asking me to read lately (some poems, a couple of chapters of the book he's working on) and also for the way he looks at me. I had not noticed either as particularly unusual. I suppose in our world, we're used to this sort of sharing and friendliness. He went on to tell me what a joy it had been when I was friendly towards him after he arrived—someone for him to relate to—but that he also found me "disconcertingly lovely." He's also picked up on my vulnerability and obviously feels somewhat protective towards me. He felt he had already done what examining of his conscience he felt necessary and believes that his enjoyment of me is not disloyal to his wife. In his telling me of his feelings, I think he thought he was (American style) clarifying our relationship, trying to ensure that I was not troubled by his attention and to reassure me that, despite his own experience of being disconcerted, it was basically a straightforward friendship. No doubt his intentions were honourable and from the best of motives.

Yet I feel angry and shaken and confused. Why am I so shaken? First, I suppose, because his "confession" came so unexpectedly, right out of the blue. With my easy-going intimacy with a number of people, I had found nothing odd in the pattern of our relating. For him, it seems, it was more exceptional. Secondly, I had been coming to value Joel as an important friend, indeed one of the very few here I feel I can really talk to about matters of faith and the intellectual life. Without my realising it, he had become like a kind of anchor for me here: safe, dependable and nourishing for me in some way. Yesterday's twenty minutes has, at a stroke, made the whole relationship— for me at least—much more complicated.

Yes, I know I am overreacting, but I now wonder about the implications of my friendship within their marriage. Their marriage is basically a good one, but as is so common in the West, I have a great deal in common with him on account of our work that his wife can't really share. She's not an academic and has largely devoted her married life to caring for the children. Which I admire. But I know from past friendships with male colleagues that this can lead to the all-too-familiar "my wife doesn't understand me" sequence. Yet I don't think Joel's response to me is quite that. But even so, I will be more self-conscious about taking initiatives. Oh shit! I can just feel myself getting all tied up in knots! Ivy, you mentioned in your last letter that many of your friends are married couples. Have you ever found yourself in this situation, of being closer to the husband than to the wife, of knowing that he was attracted to you? Is friendship possible in such circumstances?

In the wake of this new emotional upheaval, I realise that one of the things I am missing right now is good female friendship. I haven't yet seemed to be able to find the good female friendships I enjoyed in my previous place. I absolutely agree with your comments about the absence of intimate friendships, and I know that my propensity to fall in love so easily has often been due to my lack of deep connections within a culture, the difficulty, with all my moving, of establishing genuine intimacy. Having said that, one of the things I really learned to value in the States was the close friendship of strong, interesting women. Same-sex friendship is something that I don't think we are taught adequately to value in a culture that seems, as you say, to set so much store by finding a mate. Convention states that one's female friends can be let down at the drop of a hat if the offer of a hot date with an attractive male comes up. Are potential boyfriends so much more important than friends?

And what of our capacity to really be friends with someone of the opposite sex? Is this really a possibility? Or will we inevitably always view each other as potential mates? It's not that one can ever deny that one is a sexual being, nor would I want to. No doubt all our relating, whether to men or to women, has its sexual component. What I think I am lamenting is the fact that this dimension seems to have been emphasised to such an extent in Western culture that it assumes a proportion that far outweighs its real value. Its imperative skews so many relationships that could otherwise be so valuable, so straightforward, so helpful in meeting some of our legitimate needs for human intimacy.

I am thinking again of my reaction to Joel's innocent acknowledgment. There we were, two people with a great deal in common and a developing depth of affection that clearly meant a lot to us both. He begins to worry if this is inappropriate, given that he has a wife; I am shaken in case it means I have inadvertently been leading someone on. And so, a potentially wonderful friendship is suddenly inhibited by all sorts of doubts and qualifications simply because our culture teaches us that the sexual chord is the dominant one whenever a man and a woman relate. It's not that I am naive. I have seen affairs develop and marriages break up as a result of friendships that started innocently enough. But here again, it seems that the pressures of society's script may have something to do with the direction in which a relationship feels fatally compelled. In our sex-obsessed culture, what other route is there for a man and a woman who feel drawn to each other to take? But I refuse to accept that this is inevitable. That there are not alternative ways.

Again, I am struck by what you had to say about celibacy. I'm intrigued by your notion of celibacy not simply being for those who are single, but about a larger orbit of restraint, an "expansive state of being" to be pursued by all. I don't quite understand what celibacy within marriage might involve. Does it mean the total abstention of sexual relations between husband and wife? I must admit that this does sound odd to my Western ears. Yet the broad contours of what you say I believe I do understand and I wholeheartedly agree with you.

In actual fact, I wonder if Joel was attempting, however clumsily, to find a slightly alternative path in trying to address with integrity his friendship with me. I know that he and Barb have a philosophy of marriage that assumes sexual faithfulness but encourages emotional openness to others. Perhaps what he was trying to do was to establish, even risk, a depth of friendship with me that acknowledged my needs for friendship and intimacy, without going down the customary routes that such relationships between the sexes usually take. Usually we feel compelled to choose between a dangerous sexual liaison or blocking the friendship at certain levels to head off the risk of getting into deep waters. But maybe a third path is viable. Joel is clearly not blind to the element of attraction. And his confession has made me aware that I am quite deeply attracted to him. To call it sexual doesn't quite capture the sense of delight I feel for this man, for his warmth and radiance and care. It is certainly not about wanting to go to bed with him; I don't find him sexually attractive as such. But I find in me a longing to know him much better, to continue to matter to him deeply, yet all within a friendship that is quite happy to accept the boundaries of his marriage. This could be quite a challenge. I shall keep you posted!

Meantime, I am anxious to hear about your own experiences in such waters. The traditional Christian stance that tells single people simply to keep their hands off just won't do: it is equally paranoid about the sexual imperative. And surely Christians of all people should be trying to find "the more excellent way." So, how do we negotiate these paths of dangerous liaisons and innocent friendships? Write soon.

Love,
M.

हवाई पत्र
Aerogramme

Negotiating the Rapids

Boston: May 21st, 1989

Dear Margaret,

It is good that we have the phone for the immediate and letters for the extended! Your recent letter on "dangerous liaisons and innocent friendships" was a provocative one.

Again and again we keep coming back to how deeply we are written by our families, communities and cultures. As I thought about opposite-sex intimacies especially as they relate to your friend Joel, I kept coming back to some of my own approaches in these matters.

While I was growing up in India (things are changing fast these days), the sexual ethic was markedly different from what you have been exposed to. The recognition of the powerful potency of sexual energies between men and women led to the development of all sorts of social safeguards on gender relations. As I have told you before, exclusively male and female educational institutions (there were a few exceptions), gendered social gatherings, arranged marriages were some of the means employed. In my case, while I was expected to marry, it was never expected of me to find the man to marry. The absence of this expectation, in fact the strict forbiddance of it had all sorts of social implications as a female for me. I was not socialised to make myself "attractive" or "available" to men. My primary female experience of the world for over two decades meant that men did not appear as individuated entities. There was not the conscious or subconscious need to scout the field and compete for purposes of conquest. In short all this means that when I came West, I was somewhat nervous about relating to single men for fear of entanglements and felt extremely confident in my attachments with married men, for after all they were (I hoped) like my father.

Of course, I have had very interesting experiences on this front. For the most part I've had remarkably close relationships with most of these men. I did not wonder why I was closer to the men than their wives. It was often quite clear—in the world of education or work (at least the kind you and I are in), there were more men than women. You are aware of some of these relationships. You know that with my various dislikes and inabilities (going to buy a car, a house, negotiating with institutions, paying my taxes, etc.), I would be at sea without these men. I am deeply beholden to them. I suspect that the relationships have been secure because the boundaries of my relationship have been clear. Yet there was one instance where there was potential for misunderstanding from the spouse. I quickly worked on surrendering that friendship.

My thinking is that such relationships between singles and married are not frequent within the culture because there is the constant threat of crossing boundaries. In a culture where falling in love is imperative for partnerships, it is very difficult to rid yourself of those instincts/abilities even after marriage. I am amazed at the tendency of so many people to flirt unreservedly, believing that this is the only way to conduct themselves across gender lines. In Joel's comment about your being "disturbingly beautiful" he is clearly guarding himself against some other potential dynamic. It is the old story about a raging fire alongside a haystack and to think that each can rise above this power is unrealistic.

My belief is that while one pursues intellectual and spiritual exchanges in all sorts of relationships, if these interfere with existing commitments and attachments, these pursuits then should become secondary. The individuals involved should be mature enough to recognise that and bow out, instead of expecting that somehow all parties concerned are strong and free enough to carry on simultaneously. It really does vary from individual to individual I suppose. Because we have been so prescribed by our cultures, our sexual energies are ever present in all our dealings. To deny them is foolish; to recognise and regulate them one draws on other friendships and one's own convictions.

Don't overestimate your strength to resist, Margaret. The line between emotional bonds and physical bonding is very fine. In your present attraction, you will need great strength; is all the tearing and turmoil really worth it? No matter what *your* intent, you are both battling with possibilities and interpretations outside yourselves. Your comment about his confession leading you to your awareness that you are "quite deeply attracted to him" is, I think, quite telling. In other words, he has an influence (potential anyway) on you that is quite subterranean to your own consciousness. Think about it. I am not alluding to anything exclusively sexual either. I am talking about a response between the two of you that is more total and all encompassing than that. While I respect your desire to "know him much better, to continue to matter to him deeply," I also know that you want the blessing of his wife in this. It is not that she is any less in this matter, it is that there are limits to territory, as there are in all relationships. It is not merely about sexual power; it is also about respect, trust, security and boundaries.

In the end, I do believe that very close friendships can be had between the sexes, but each does well to consider the sexual component rather than overlook it. I think that my "resident alien" identity has been to my advantage: people seem to have respect/confidence in my cultural allegiances and therefore carry the implicit expectation that I am safe. Yet I myself seem to be drawn to "safe" men—those who are either married or gay. And I have made some intimate connections among them.

I don't know if this has been helpful. I'd like to know what you think.

Love,
Ivy

Stormy Seas

England: May 30th, 1989

Dear Ivy,

Your latest letter was sobering. Parts of it told me what I did not want to hear. I suppose you're warning me to be very careful with regard to my friendship with Joel, and that, despite the good intentions of us both, and despite the fact that I do not believe anything even close to an affair is a remote possibility, I must be cautious.

I was very interested to read about your own account of your friendships with married couples, and I suppose I must concede that your own cultural preparation and expectations do indeed prepare you better than I have been for negotiating such relationships. Or at least they clarify the boundaries more clearly and therefore make misunderstandings and unwise entanglements less likely. Nevertheless, I am reluctant to concede that a third way—an alternative to either inappropriate intimacy or simply blocking a potential friendship—is not sometimes viable.

And yet, even as I write, I am aware that, since Joel's conversation with me—two weeks ago now—I have found our friendship much harder to negotiate. I feel as if I'm trying to pilot a ship through stormy waters without a compass. Certainly, our friendship has lost its uncomplicated innocence and spontaneity, and I feel constantly on guard. I'm not sure how aware he is of the shift or of the small tidal wave he has set in motion within me. Maybe scarcely at all. With term in full flood, there have been plenty of good reasons why he might think I am simply too busy to linger over coffee. For my part, I have to admit that there are dangers. I have grown more aware, even in this last fortnight that, however good and uncomplicated Joel may well be in himself, there are indeed forces and patterns outside ourselves that we will be forced to reckon with. I am not unaware of a general pattern of middle-aged men being susceptible to younger women as the balance of their own marriages has gradually changed; I am equally aware of my own susceptibility to sympathetic father figures. And I am conscious of the potential dangers of sharing a world in common—intellectual, but also geographical—that his wife cannot share. I've met the "my wife doesn't understand me" scenario before, and although Joel never hinted at this, I realise that our friendship might inadvertently develop in ways that might exclude her despite our efforts. (I remember feeling a little aware of this at that dinner party: was she able to be part of the conversation enough? Was it too "in-house," too academic?) So, although nothing "untoward" will ever happen between us, I am aware of the scope for unnecessary emotional turmoil, and perhaps this is danger enough.

I find I am now acutely conscious of this man; my feelings about him, now that they have been aroused, are obviously not those of uncomplicated friendship. I am very sensitive to his presence in a room: I am simultaneously excited and nervous and find it hard to behave spontaneously without feeling unduly self-conscious, trying to calculate the effect of what anything will be on him, or what onlookers might inadvertently pick up in the way we relate to each other. It is immensely infuriating, and I find myself going to considerable lengths to avoid him and not to have to deal with all this heightened consciousness. I suppose, as you detected, I am experiencing a kind of infatuation or form of "in loveness" in which my feelings are very hard to control. They still do not have a dominant sexual tone. I just find myself deeply drawn to this man, and touched that he finds me beautiful. It's as if he radiates the warmth and beauty of a candle flame, and I just long to be near him to enjoy him and his enjoyment of me. Yet I fear self-immolation. I am frightened and disappointed in what feels like my intense vulnerability in all this. A man just has to tell me he finds me beautiful and I fall for him? I'm nearly thirty years old, for God's sake, and yet I feel as pathetic as a thirteen-year-old in her first infatuation. The only difference is I know I am much better at hiding my feelings and behaving as I should, even if my feelings won't! It's a real struggle but, despite the turmoil, I do feel clearer about some of the issues at stake. Thank you for your honesty and your caution.

I have found it helpful, as you suggested, to think more about how Barb might feel about a close friendship between myself and Joel. In fact, I have thought about this quite a lot. She and I are unlikely ever to get to know each other that well, and even if friendship between us were geographically possible, I don't think we have a huge amount in common. Certainly nowhere as much as Joel and I have. I don't know if he has told her about his "confession" two weeks ago, but I'm trying to imagine how I would feel in her shoes if it were my husband abroad, spending quite a bit of time talking with a young single colleague with whom he had a great deal in common and to whom he also felt attracted (crass word: the poverty of our vocabulary!). And who was attracted back. With the best will in the world, and no matter how much I trusted him—and her—I might still well feel pangs of jealousy and vulnerability.

So, feeling somewhat battered in the storm, I find myself withdrawing from the lofty and perhaps overoptimistic aspirations of my last letter. Certainly at the moment, I don't have the strength to maintain the close friendship we had. I shall stick to the traditional route of keeping the friendship at a slight distance and work at getting my unruly emotions back into order. I must confess, I am still angry that he had to make the whole thing explicit. I do think that it would have been quite possible to maintain the friendship we did have, especially given the fact that he will be heading back to the States in a month or so. No doubt his motives were of the best, but it feels as if he has cleared his conscience at the expense of dumping too much responsibility onto me. Bloody men! Equally, I'm fed up with myself that I couldn't handle it.

I still wonder how possible friendship is between the sexes in the West. You comment on the early socialisation of us Westerners to find a mate, and the difficulty, once this has been accomplished, in suddenly changing our responses to the opposite sex when the relationship we are seeking is not a sexual one. If you are right, then perhaps it is inevitably harder for me than it is for you to have the kind of friendship with a married man that I would like. I'm still reluctant to concede this in principle. What I do realise is that I do not possess a vocabulary for powerful emotion in friendship with someone of the opposite sex.

I have been thinking quite a lot about the whole notion of friendship lately, partly, no doubt, prompted by the fact that I feel slightly lonely here still. It is still early days, and the friendships I am beginning to make are still nascent; they cannot yet carry the weight of what you and I have, for example. I recently started Aelred of Rievaulx's *On Friendship* and am finding it compelling reading. Even though it was written some nine hundred years ago, there is a remarkable immediacy about the writing, and something immensely gentle and winsome about the personality that comes through.

In particular, I think I am impressed and surprised at the very high value he places on human friendship. One tends to think of monks living long ago in often austere conditions, cutting themselves off from all human attachments and rather frowning on something as human as friendship. Yet Aelred places such a high value on friendship that he describes it as a kind of preparation, a practice, if you like, for our friendship with God.

It is a very high view of friendship that I think we have largely lost these days. In the States, as here, I am struck by the fear some of my students feel in revealing their troubles and wounds and inadequacies to their friends. Below the apparent openness and friendliness of the culture, there is the real fear that people will reject them if they know how bad they really are. I wonder if it is also connected with the professionalisation of counseling. No doubt there are many good and valuable— even vital—things about this service. But I can't help wondering if in our modern tendency to see this as the solution to so many emotional problems, too much is lost. Perhaps people grow to think too easily that their friend "needs counseling" when what is really needed is the love and support of a listening ear, of a friend who can help to carry the burden of pain. Not all problems are soluble. Do we grow to assume in this late twentieth century of ours that they are, and therefore to find the burden of helping to carry a friend's pain intolerable?

So much of our identity is forged in being able to tell our story to sympathetic others. How important it is to be able simply to recount the events of the day to someone who cares about us; no doubt it is our way of making sense of them, of developing a narrative that helps to shape us and define us. I am certain that such sharing, both apparently superficial, but also on much deeper levels, is absolutely crucial to our mental well-being. Do you think that the over sexualisation of our culture has diverted us from this vital form of intimacy, which usually occurs between friends of the same gender? Are we being subtly programmed to think that all significant social occasions must contain both sexes to be really significant, to be worthy of our serious engagement and attention?

I can still remember a wonderful dinner party with some of my women friends in the States. The food and wine were good, but it was the quality of the talk, the ambience, the quality of intimacy within the context of rigorous debate that was so special. The thought suddenly struck me that the evening was perfect; to have had a man there would have changed its energy, and even spoiled it in some way. This feeling struck me almost with the force of a revelation, so contrary was it to what so many young Western women—including myself—are taught to believe: that the success of social intercourse needs men to be complete. It wasn't that I thought "Who needs men?" or something like that. As you know, I am rather partial to men's company! It was rather the realisation that I had discovered more deeply than ever before the richness of women's fellowship and friendship. I'm sure men also need time to be with other men, not always to be defined in terms of their relationships with women...which almost inevitably involves being aware of one's identity as a sexual being. Again, there's nothing wrong with this as such, but too often it seems to be our only way of relating, of interpreting, of defining our identity.

Have we in the West lost the capacity for passionate, intimate, even intense but nonsexual same-sex friendship? Is a friendship like ours so unusual? I know that others have speculated about us: "Are you lesbians?" they wonder, when we speak of our joy in each other, when our lives, even oceans apart, seem so intimately bound up in each other's. When I teach

Tennyson's *In Memoriam*, that great Victorian elegy with its heartbreaking lament for a dead friend, students automatically seem to assume that Tennyson must have been gay. He uses such intimate language, borrowing the vocabulary of marriage quite unselfconsciously to try to find words and images to convey how bereft he feels at the death of his dearest friend. What concerns me is not so much whether or not Tennyson was gay (I think not, but I'm sure there are other scholars who will argue that clearly he was just repressing it), but that our generation in the West seems to have lost a vital category: are we only able to imagine relationships that are primarily sexual? Is there no vocabulary for intimate same-sex friendship? This imperialism of the sexual is worrying (and I speak as one who often feels conquered): it frustrates me that all our longing for intimacy must be focused on a sexual partner. This burden is surely intolerable.

Ivy, what do you think of all this? Is there more space made for female friendship in Indian culture? I am sure there is. I would be interested to hear about your own thoughts on friendship.

Love,
Margaret

On Friendship

Dear Margaret,

Thanks again for the previous letter. I am no longer fearful about your challenge with the Joel-Barb relationship. Despite your present pain and the confusion of your feelings, I know you will work it out.

I am struck by your recollection of the all-women dinner party you attended. My mind was on "rewind" as I reread that bit. Indeed, it is an aspect of Indian social life that I sorely miss. After a lifetime of extremely intimate female friendships, I felt cheated once again by the adult world I came to be part of. As I have told you before, there were no "girlfriends" or "boyfriends"; just friends, and they were all girls. Interminable phone conversations, spending days and nights together, picnics, family excursions, letter writing, sharing food, clothes, books, tutoring each other and private conversations were the order of my day. And there was the heartache—the fighting, the jealousies, the competition, the conceit. Did this belong to an erstwhile childhood and youth, or could they be had in later years? I don't know. I do know that many of my wonderful friendships were rudely interrupted by marriage, and I have lost most of my friends. Somehow, there is a native quality about the intimacies between women that cannot be had with men. At some inexplicable level, there is no need for explanations and introductions; instinct is all. I long for those possibilities again, but the world in the West is structured so differently. If one was to find such friendships, I would imagine that they would act as a great buffer for some of the messy cross-gender connections that people often seem to get into. The loss of female friendships is not only a personal loss but also a cultural loss for me. Being in touch with people is very important to me. I am not sure if this need is exaggerated for me since I am so far from home; in any case it is made especially hard in the absence of female friends who are free of attachments.

I am also struck by cultural perceptions of same-gender friendships in the West. In most of the cities in Asia and Africa I have seen a display of same-gender camaraderie—men and men, women and women are laughing, holding hands, walking arm in arm. Such affection is conspicuously absent in the West. When there is a show of such affection, it is necessarily homosexual and is seen as taboo. Consequently it seems as if the heterosexuals, for fear of being identified as homosexual, refrain from intimacy with members of their own sex. There seems to be an implicit cultural assumption that "normal" involves either an absence of emotion and physical affection where one is seen as self-contained and self-controlled, or an excessive display of both with some significant other of the opposite sex. What a shame! (I don't know if you recall one snowy Sunday morning as we got out of our car to walk towards the church, I tried to hold your arm for support on the ice, and you gave me your arm sparingly, and I remember thinking about the gender bit and all the attendant social taboos. Were I a man, the response would have been quite different!) I can't help but think that to some extent such behaviour stems from the compulsive heterosexist culture the West has become. Social intimacy must be strictly *hetero* and *sexual*. Such expectation is a marvelous recipe for distortions among heterosexuals and those outside the loop.

Recently, I was surprised with a phone call from Helena Anderson. One night out of the blue she was ringing to ask me rather bluntly if you and I were lesbian. I was taken aback by this and disappointed that our friendship should be construed in such a way. Have people in the West lost the imagination to believe that close, intimate same-sex friendships are possible? And yet such (nonsexual) friendships are by no means uncommon. A similar thing happened to a friend (who now lives in Iran) and me once before. This person couldn't understand how Lila and I were in constant company.

Perhaps I am naive, but I am perplexed by the endless power of sex in the West. The sensual self reigns supreme. Social theorists note that these states arise from the alienation, atomisation and anomie that societies go through while in flux. All the materialistic avarice for food, drink, dance, music, travel, art, home technology, etc., etc., that is so seductive in Western life is so contrary to the miserable groveling for the material that the poor of this world are put to. Against such affluence, there is an emergence of poverty—the sheer idolatry of the human body, human sexual prowess, sexual identity and relationships. Does material affluence lead to the oversexualisation of the human body in keeping with the general commodification of most life? Is it again due to the bankruptcy of all else? I know that it wasn't always so. Your references to Tennyson, Shakespeare's *Sonnets* (was it?) and all the many other literary expressions of close same-gender friendships attest to another age.

Why are all sorts of other relationships less appealing? My heart goes out to the men even more because they seem less free than women are on this matter. I wonder how much of this is tied up with our ideas of independence and "real manhood?" So "real" men appear to stand on their own, needing little and no one. Women and children are merely trophies for their independent standing. In turn "real women" look for men to relate to. Mr. Right becomes her focus, while other relationships are looked on as somewhat specious. What does such pressure do to those outside such heterosexist, patriarchal machinations?

I recently read a moving essay in an anthology on human sexuality. It was called "A Rose for Julia"; the writer talked about an event in her early childhood when she was going to a school party. Earlier in the day she had got her mother to buy her a rose for the party. She wanted to give the rose to her lovely friend Julia, whom she adored. While driving her to the party her mother asked her who she was giving the rose to. Her mother was enraged when she found out that the rose was for Julia. How inappropriate for girls to be giving flowers to other girls; she should have set her affections for boys at the party, the writer was told. The rose was impounded from the little girl and it turned out to be a crushing evening. As I read this, I was shocked at the absurdity of such social expectations that are ever so explicit.

Parents often chuckle with satisfaction and relief at their young children's interests in children of the opposite sex. Not only is this seen as a mark of the child's maturation and normalcy, but there is also a laissez-faire attitude on the part of families to provide instruction on the potent powers of human sexuality. Such socialisation reaps its distortions in later years. I am particularly sad that there are no allowances whatsoever for the integration of sexuality into celibacy. In the event that there are, such people are largely seen as "weird" or "dangerous," and are looked at with reservation.

I am by no means laying the burden of responsibility and change on parents, schools or other social institutions. After all, they are all agents of culture. The effects of industrialisation, capitalism and modernity on culture need closer examination in order to gain some handle on present situations. The imperative of hypermasculinity, which the market demands in all sorts of tangible and intangible ways, affects the deepest human sensibilities among men and women. In the end we inevitably become hypercapitalists, even in the affairs of our heart. We commodify the body and sexual pleasure, we disregard any communal responsibility when it comes to our romantic pursuits, we count on our personal powers to attract and to hold. Divorce remains a solution to any inefficiency in the marriage. Through it all, our individual selves reign supreme. How we pay for the distortion of a wonderful gift from God!

Thinking of gifts, I know what we have is a gift and I thank God that we were prepared to receive it. Margaret, I can't wait to see you in the summer. In fact I am pretty sure that I will come, as I have reason to go home again (yes, my mother is lining the men up again. But more on that in a few minutes). I was thinking of visiting the Vanderpols in Amsterdam. In fact we've talked about it. Would you like to go with me? It would be great fun if you could. When does your term end? If you are interested, it is not too early to check up on the plane fares; and if it's too much we can think of the ferry. In any case let me know so that I can make plans.

Yes, once again my mother has written that she has one and a half men ready for my perusal. The first is some priest (she is of course appealing to my religious sensibilities now) and the other is an academic who is only half interested (that's why I say that he is half and my mother thinks that the half will unfold to full upon my arrival). In the meanwhile word has got out among relatives here that I might be going to India, so they have thrown in one of their eligibles for my consideration. The total is two and a half. This last one is a doctor (not a psychiatrist I hope!). I know most about him from his relatives here;

the others I will know more about when I get there. Margaret, I'll write/tell you more. Take care.

Love,
Ivy

Sexual Iconoclasts!

England: June 15th, 1989

Dear Ivy,

So, Helena wondered if we were lesbians, did she! In a way, it doesn't surprise me. After all, our friendship is more intense than most others I know. Perhaps because we started our friendship in the States as single women far from our families, we quickly assumed the role of "significant other" for each other. As I hinted in my last letter, I grow more convinced that sharing our lives with others, with close friends and family, with the people we know are *for* us, who want to know the details of the unfolding of our days and lives, is crucial for our human well-being. I have been immensely grateful—and particularly when I was so far away from my family in the U.S.—to know that there was someone I could count on to rejoice with me in my successes and joys and to mourn with me in my failures and losses. To have someone who had the privilege of "interfering," of offering advice unsolicited, who knew what I was doing from week to week, if not from day to day…all this I have been able to count on in our friendship, and for this I am deeply grateful.

I have noticed, too, that, for whatever reason, we are both

more likely to want to tell people about each other than is common. Part of it is the fact that we are quite an integral part of each other's life, and so the other comes up naturally in a number of conversations. But for me there is also the sense of amazement that I have found such a friend, the real gratitude that I have an Ivy in my life. It is a joy and wonder that I find myself sharing with others, much as one does when one wants to tell friends about a fascinating teacher or writer or boyfriend. It's the human instinct to want to share what is so good, as well as what is so bad, to want to tell others of what is out of the ordinary in one's life. I have noticed that you do the same: when I meet your friends and colleagues, I know by their reaction to me that they are aware of the significance of our friendship. They often tell me as much.

Yet it is sad if the only way some people can interpret this is by assuming that we are gay! It is not that I am offended by such an assumption—at least I hope I am not. No, it is rather what we have spoken of already, the poverty of our modern interpretation of relationship that can only understand intense, close friendship in terms of a sexual relationship. It is like having available a huge orchestra of every conceivable instrument, and the conductor only ever inviting the brass section to play. Have we lost the subtlety of appreciating all the other variations and combinations and possibilities in the spectrum of human relating? Have we forgotten that three quarters of the instruments lie silent? Is it to the insistent notes of sex alone that we now listen?

No doubt our desire is shaped and manipulated by all the advertising we absorb each day, with its cynical knowledge that sex sells. I sometimes wonder if gay people can duck out of some of this, aimed so heavily as it all is toward heterosexual couples and happy families. Homosexuals at least force us to question whether or not such ideals are as inevitable, as normal, as desirable as they are made out to be. You speculate about the connection between gay identity and the desire to eschew the dominant elements in patriarchal heterosexual culture. Being forced themselves to seek alternatives in a heterosexual world, I also think that they help all of us, potentially, to be more aware of the falseness of the idols we so compulsively pursue. Sexual iconoclasts! We certainly need some major surgery!

Next to you, I think it is my gay friends who have made me think most about the way I see human intimacy as expressed in our culture. Time and again, they push me to question what I take for granted, to interrogate the pressures and supposed "norms" of our deeply heterosexualised world. And when I catch a glimpse into all the added complications of forging partnerships with someone of one's own sex, given all the cultural taboos that still operate, I begin to wonder how any survive at all!

So, some more suitors in the pipeline for you! It seems a while since last you had to go through the vetting procedure. I thought you had decided to give up on it and pursue a life of glorious celibacy!

I would love to join you in your visit to Amsterdam. I know the Vanderpols a little and would welcome the chance to get to know them better. And besides, there is a marvelous Van Gogh exhibition in Amsterdam just now. It would be the perfect opportunity to see that. And I will be ready for a little break from England by then, I'm sure. I'll be in touch with you by phone regarding our travel details and specific dates as soon as I've managed to make some enquiries. Take care, Ivy.

Love,
M.

R eading back over this section of our correspondence, I am aware of how often significant growth is accompanied by difficult trials. So often, one takes three steps forward and, just as one is congratulating oneself on the achievement, something throws a spanner in the works and one finds oneself sliding right back to the beginning.

I think this is how it felt over the few months of these last letters. I can feel again the liberating sense of discovery, of wrestling with new options, or options not yet taken fully seriously—celibacy, friendship and other such sources of strength and inspiration beyond simply seeking refuge in matrimony as the most obvious solution to one's aloneness or lack of self- and societal definition. I remember those months as very serene and exciting, with a new sense of possibility and peace and joy as I tried to step off the whirligig of romance.

The friendship with Joel [not, of course, his real name] threw me off balance. I was confused about what to do with a friendship that seemed at once so nourishing and yet so fraught with danger. I am still not at all sure about our conclusions in this debate about friendship between single and married people of the opposite sex. With the benefit of distance, and with the emotions that shook me then long since settled, I still wonder if there could not be a better way to negotiate such dilemmas. Indeed, since then, I have seen others tread such waters with much greater success than seemed possible for me, and from this I take encouragement.

Friendship—with each other, and with many others—has continued to be a source of great delight and strength to each of us, and the determination to take seriously its commitments and obligations has deepened. Without a doubt, such bonds are of vital importance in a world in which so many of the family networks that our ancestors took for granted exist no longer. And each of us continues to reflect on the challenges and possibilities of the celibate life, which was touched on fairly scantily in our correspondence.

Neither of us is competent to address issues concerned with being homosexual in a heterosexual world. We have some inkling of the experience from gay friends who have to struggle far more than we must to find viable ways of living in relationship in this homophobic world of ours. From such friends we have gained much inspiration and courage as we have watched them try to forge new paths where none are in existence. Their task is both harder and easier than ours. Because culture is largely hostile to gay men and women, they are forced in many ways to live on the margins, aware too often that they are aliens in a strange land.

So, where have we reached on this journey? Back to the letters. Things are about to change dramatically in our lives. We have criticised and bemoaned our respective cultural entrammelments for long enough! One of us is about to break out into a new phase and into the first real attempt to be guided by positive reappropriations and remouldings of the values once discarded....

PART THREE

Courtship

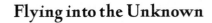

Flying into the Unknown

Midair: July 20th, 1989

Dear Margaret,

Leaving the Vanderpols in Amsterdam and you at the tube station when you set off for Taizé was very hard for me. I am writing this on the plane, and I have never felt so far from you and even fear that I may not see you again. Terrible thought! It may just be that I am older, but I sense something ominous in the air. It is as if all that I have fought for all my life is going to evaporate into thin air one of these days, and I will be reduced to nothing. Confusion and ambivalence are the real words that I am trying to hedge putting down. I don't know, I feel my will dissipating—not unlike the way I felt fifteen years ago when I was being pressured to marry. What is of course different and disturbing now is that I feel that the power is going out of me. Then I had more confidence; now I am not sure at all. I feel spent, like a child's music box that is unwinding itself into the silence of the night.

I miss you very much now. While I am well aware of how distant and alien my cultural circumstances are from your own, I have never once felt judged for our differences. I am so grateful for that. Even in my present moment of alienation from my own self, you are a living presence in my mind and I take some comfort in that. I can't imagine a future without you. And yet, there could very well be one if life is not kind. What do I mean?

There is a parade of human characters going through my mind just now. My parents, who saw each other in the company of their families for twenty minutes prior to their wedding day. My friend Sheila, who had been betrothed to her maternal uncle ever since she was an infant. Mala's paternal aunt and maternal uncle, who were married to each other. My brother and his wife, who affirmed each other in holy matrimony after spending six hours with each other. This was a generous length of time considering the going privileges for other couples. None were "in love." This was my native world.

I grew up hearing my mother recount the most inspiring love story of her younger days—the abdication of the British throne by King Edward VIII, all for the love of an American divorcée, Wallis Simpson. Perhaps she marveled at the absurdity of such romantic reasoning for anyone at all, but all the more so for the King of England! I don't know. In any case, it was all quite wondrous and magical for new adults like my peers and myself. After all, there was no such excitement to our own families. For myself, the fantasies spun in love stories were far more appealing than the sterile and insipid marriages my friends were entering.

Then, I was convinced that I was going to fight for my life if I had to, before I succumbed to this fossilised idea of submitting to a stranger forever. There was something special about being sought out for the self that one possessed, for styles and substances unique to one's own being. You wanted to know and be known, to become the subject of someone's desires. After all, even God knows you this way presumably.

Today I live with twin inheritances. The perennial seeds of choice and possibilities that were planted in me by my family (in my early days at home) and nurtured by the romance novels that I read. I have also been surrounded by the cultural deference to active family and community responsibility and involvement in the arrangement and blessing of marriages in India. But as I think about it, these creative dimensions of our cultures have gone so terribly wrong. What do I do with a mottled life such as mine? Behind the labyrinth of culture in the East and the West lie some similarities that are troubling. Regardless of the agency of the individual or the community, there is a strong contractual nature to these marriage arrangements. Love and commitment seem to be scarce in both cases. The contractual dimension to these unions is highly private, confined to the immediate family. There is little consideration of the consequences of the marriage in the weave of the larger social fabric. It is the neglect of the social implications of marriage among the parties involved that is threatening the institution itself. In the West, marriages break down partly because the mates involved carry too much of the responsibility for making it work. Expectations are high, and there is little recourse outside of the self except with professional counselors. In the East, expectations of each other are few to nonexistent, and the marriages work as if on automatic pilot. Lives, especially of wives, are turning to still-life forms. Is it possible to forge a via media through these two worlds?

While I have never been one who *lives* to marry, for a long time now I have been convicted by the notion that *all* our undertakings should enhance our living in this world. Both our cultures have been dangerously misled into focusing exclusively on the nuclear facets of marriage—the overriding concern is about "suitability" for "self." Surely this is not what is sacramental about the knot in our tie. Rather, it's all about the multiplicity of ties generated by this nuptial knot. So instead of our narrow concern about whether or not the couple is compatible, or "made for each other" or "in love," should we and they not be asking: What good is this marriage for the world? Is the world a better place for this union? Has a new day dawned for the cause of love, justice and peace? The sacrament is desacralised when class, education, family, vocation, religion and daily life are turned inward and the circle is drawn around the self.

Marriage ought to facilitate self in community. In this sense, my primary allegiances, whether in a married or single state, must not be altered. Yes, marriage and family are riddled with all sorts of compromises, and I think of that scripture that suggests that the ideal state for the sake of service is the single state. In the end, if my partnership in marriage is not aligned with my prior partnership with God and the world, I will come to grief. It is these matters that I am fearful and prayerful about now. While marriage has the potential for transcendence and grandeur, it is, in too many marriages, the imperative of the pragmatic that guides the day. Such settlement is a frightening possibility.

My mind now is in overdrive as it always is in the face of an impending suitor-meeting. It is a funny energy, this. You perhaps think that I have bid adieu to an arranged marriage, so why the worry now? In a recent discussion on arranged marriages, a group of feminists looked askance at me. It is actually more complicated and less cut and dried than common perception would have it. I have never really put the possibility of marriage out of my mind. Considering the force of socialisation, you can imagine that it has always been a lingering factor in my life. The only difference is that in recent years I have felt a bit more in control. For one thing I feel less and less like I am under the spell of family or culture (except every time I am on a plane homeward bound). I have been able to have a long-distance perspective on India, and it provides me with some objectivity. It certainly helps that I am older, reasonably independent, and with a coterie of friends who care very much for me. Most importantly, my time in the West has been sufficiently long enough to rid myself of any illusions I might have had about the prospects there.

When I first arrived, I saw myself as being in a sort of forced and chosen exile. I then took the opportunity to explore the enticing dazzle of love and romance in the West. Mostly, I observed people in and out of love and marriage to examine the marvels of Cupid. I came to find that love was an occasional, if not an elusive, tenant here. I felt betrayed again. I had taken my life to the very edge for something I believed in and hoped for, not only for me but for all the daughters and sons yet to marry. Now, I began to wonder if I had been duped. I was stunned by the synonymous dimensions of love and lust.

Throughout human history it appears that human desire has been mistaken for human love. The culture of romance certainly feeds off of this conflation. This easy fusion of the two can perhaps be understood in the context of our "fallen" state. The state of Love is of a higher order than the state of Desire, and at the core of it love between two people exemplifies all Love and moves us to approximate the love of God itself. Love is about troth—promise, attentiveness, deep passion that manifests itself through caring and anger, the expansion of self through the surrender of self. Longing and Desire can stem from this Love. Even as I write this I am keenly aware of the tenuousness of the distinction I make—for our mortal states besieged by the ephemeral culture around us seduce us to "Desire" and not to "Love," to control and to possess rather than to free. Our intentions are often mixed, unclear and impure, and hence it may be that we never "achieve" Love—perhaps we experience it in its fleeting fugitive states here and there, now and then. Nevertheless, we can attest to having known of its wholesomeness, its rightness, its life-giving and life-expanding potential within ourselves and the other. Life is a quest for the permeation of this experience in all aspects of our being. I have certainly witnessed this in my relations with family, friends, students and others. I certainly know it in part with you. The challenge of loving lies in recognising that it is a constant questing after that which can be facilitated only through a reflective and considered implosion and explosion of self in the world.

For all the openness and accessibility in human interaction facilitated by culture and technology, I found the extent of gender stratification in the West staggering. Conformity and convention were subtly but strictly assumed, and the rhetoric of "freedom" was further perplexing. I see people desolate and desiccated, *outside* community and hence needing to rush into relationships sexually and emotionally. The East-West contrasts are compelling. At home I was struck by the primary identity of the individual as *a member* of the community and the attendant constraints therefore. In the West, I saw individual license *apart* from community. Neither culture facilitated people to be *in* community. Both peoples seemed insulated from full humanity. The consequences of social relations among men and women in the West are such that each is left to their own devices to chart codes of propriety and morality.

It is in the face of such realities that I am willing to hold a requiem for the love I sought in the West and look for a reveille of my own heritage. For the first time, I feel that I might be able to reconsider some of my options that I heretofore closed on. Having said these things, I have no idea how I will react when I get there. I suppose I am most shaken by the shifts in my own stances. Radical decisions of the past seem to be on the verge of being overturned by radical decisions yet again, and there is a real aloneness in this. Few Westerners understand, and if Easterners were to be let in (like my friends or family in India), I am terrified that they will pounce on the opportunity to appropriate my openness for their own interests and I will be no better off than I was fifteen years ago. In many ways, Margaret, I am penning a cri de coeur here. No doubt I am undergoing a crisis in meaning. Surely God knows. I hope so.

In the meanwhile there are my aging parents to think about. I wonder how they feel about their "unfinished duty," which is me. I wonder if I don't have an obligation to them. I don't know. I'll cross these bridges when I get there. It's funny how we live in so many worlds at the same time and how alone we are in each of them.

I'll discontinue this one. We're due to land in an hour or so and gradually the darkened, silent cabin is coming back to life. It has been good to feel in touch with you through these lonely hours, which feel so full of foreboding and wondering and the sense that my life is about to change forever in a way I cannot fully fathom or control. Please hold me up in your thoughts as the hour of reckoning draws nigh. Thanks for being there— especially as I have rewound and fast forwarded this long and winding life of mine. I am sending this to Montpellier, hoping that you receive it before the conference is over.

Love,
Ivy

Letter from Taizé

Dear Ivy,

Here I am in a monastery in the middle of France, sitting in the gloom of my barrackslike dormitory room at Taizé, wondering how you are. It's only five days since we said farewell at that tube station in London; by now you will be back home in Madras with your family. Is it as hard as you thought it was going to be? Has the pressure begun?

I am very grateful for the time we had together with the Vanderpols in Holland. Yet it has also left me quite worried for you. I have never seen you like that before: so fearful, so unsure of your ability to resist unwanted pressure. You said that if you did marry in India this summer, we should not get in touch with you again; it would signify the end of your old life and the start of something so completely different that it would be impossible for you to carry on old friendships. That hurt a great deal, both the sense of your own entrapment, and the thought of losing your friendship. I very much hope you were being melodramatic, even though I know your tears and fears were utterly genuine. For these reasons you are very much in my prayers, and I have never been so anxious to hear from you.

We have now been two days here at Taizé, and where better than this centre of international ecumenism and reconciliation to hold you up in prayer? My friend Anna and I had a very straightforward journey down here, and we arrived at about 7 P.M. It's been really good to catch up with her and hear all the news from the States. She's also great fun and we have laughed a lot. After the rigours of the term, that's already been immensely refreshing. The first service was amazing. It's more foreign, more different, more beautiful than I expected, and Anna is enthralled. There's the danger, of course, that we get high on the "energy" and experience and adventure rather than centering on Christ. That, of course, is what I want to aim for here: to be open to God, nourished and strengthened the more to serve and love and leave behind some of my self-centred desires.

I'll be praying for you especially, Ivy, as you try to untangle some of your own sense of what your life should be and the questions you were posing in Amsterdam of whether you expect too much. That's such a difficult question. On the one hand, as Christians, we're encouraged to expect all things and need the faith and endurance to move beyond the mediocre for others and ourselves. But this can so easily be self-centred. Here's a thought for today from Sr. Agnes. I'm not sure what I make of it but it relates to your question about demanding too much from life. The Bible passage was Matthew 6:14–21, about storing up treasure in heaven. She said, "What can it mean to attach myself so much to life that it goes beyond the limits of life…that I love so much that I choose it for all eternity?" She's trying to get away from the idea of world-denying detachment to the concept of such an intense attachment that it breaks the bounds of this life; it cannot be contained by this world and so bursts through beyond it into a kind of detachment. I'm not sure if she's right, but it would be nice to think so, especially for people like you and me with our "greedy for life" temperaments.

I'm in a discussion group with folk from all over the place—Germans, Finnish, Swedes and a Tanzanian couple. The exciting events in Eastern Europe are very evident here. It's fascinating listening to young Europeans talking together about politics, music, faith. In the Bible discussion groups, it is wonderful to see how we all help each other understand God better—especially, I think, the Tanzanians, whose perspective is the most different. They are concerned by Western self-indulgent individualism, including that which permeates our relationship with God. One or two of their comments have given me much to ponder. They were concerned today by the notion that God creates each of us individually. No, they say, he creates us as a people. They were also concerned by the idea that it doesn't matter so very much if other people/our community does not love us as long as God does. They were challenging the notion put forward by one of the Western speakers that our identity is given by God. To detach human identity from community in this way was clearly utterly alien to them and made the Westerners amongst us think again about the overpious, transcendent supracommunal God we worship. How vital it is to listen to those who see things differently in order to get some sense of where our own blind spots are.

Friday: My last night at Taizé! I'm quite sorry to leave. It's been wonderful, but not altogether for the reasons I expected. We have laughed a great deal. I think suddenly being in a place where I don't feel responsible has made me feel a little giddy, and Anna is certainly immense fun to be with! We have met some delightful people, and in a place like this you make friends very quickly, partly because you are at a place like this to start with and there's quite a lot you can take for granted. Believe it or not—of course you will—that even on this, my sabbatical within a sabbatical from men (my return to the UK was meant to be the first, if you remember!), I have had to resist a budding flirtation! Fortunately, the gentleman concerned spoke very little English and I only a little German, so his main attempts to attract attention consisted of the usual stuff—holding my gaze across a crowded tent, borrowing a pen, charming smiles. In a way, it was quite funny, although I must confess that I was a little irritated with the distraction. Earlier this evening, we tried our first conversation—for as long as our language held out. And then I said farewell and know I will never see him again. I travel on to the conference in Montpellier tomorrow, so will post this now in the hope that it reaches you before too long. No doubt it will cross with the one you are sending to me there.

I very much hope you are OK. I can imagine you feeling rather low and alone just now. Yet, despite your bleakness when last we met, I have faith that you will not give in to anything that violates your integrity. I just cannot imagine that, even though I have some sense of the pressure you feel under. I think the key thing to remember is: don't act out of fear; such motivation would lead to inauthentic choice, and despite your mother's view, "What's forty years in the light of eternity?", in reality, it would feel like a hell of a long time. I'm enclosing this Taizé cross, which I hope you like and might enjoy wearing sometimes. Among other things, it reflects my prayers for you. I bought an identical one for myself. Take care, my dear friend.

Love,
M.

Reconsiderations

Dear Margaret:

Our letters clearly crossed. Your letter from Taizé has just arrived. God knows that I found waiting for it interminable. Your extrasensory powers must have picked up on my now distraught being.

I hope you are right—that I am only being a little melodramatic. Perhaps so. I remember that time when I almost drowned in Kenya. I was taking in water fast; I had come up to the surface two or three times knowing that I wouldn't for much longer (Have I told you about this incident—about the man jumping in to save me, etc.?). What I discovered about myself then was that I was exceedingly calm and resigned, letting the elements of nature take their course. Do you know that I didn't yell for help once? While I have screamed my way through life, in the face of death I gave out. There probably was some pride there but it was mostly resignation. That's how I feel now, battling human nature, my own and that of others—resigned and terrified. Any instinct to survive is dissipating fast.

So much of what I am going through has to do with some radical shifts in my own sensibilities. Time and distance have moved me to a different place now, and I feel like I am on a new frontier, one that potentially involves someone else. Actually, I even feel somewhat indulgent about the troubles I seem to heap over myself. My questions are nonquestions for everyone else here. Why am I so important? Why are **my** freedoms, choices and happiness so primary? There is something prophetic and sagacious about my mother's statement, "What's thirty or forty years in light of eternity?" This seemingly philosophical comment is really a cultural comment on the individual in the cosmic scheme. This is very much in keeping with your discussion with the Tanzanian couple at Taizé—God creates us as a **people**. Blood links are crucial to abstract a sense of selfhood. The material self is a significant self. This was what I have been keenly missing in the best love stories of the West—this concentric location of self rooted in family, community, country, the world and the universe finally. The stories were all void of a corporate identity. Yes, I am well aware that the sense of communities rooted in land, lineage, blood, craft, creed and such have passed away in industrialised societies; I am also aware that many people in the West are earnestly in search of some form of social cement to provide identity.

I remember being veritably moved to tears at seeing Nick Vanderpol kneeling down to pray the Lord's Prayer in Dutch while we worshiped in Amsterdam. I know that for Nick to be able to pray in Dutch was to be in authentic connection and celebration of his own heritage although he was himself a second-generation American. The universality of a distant God's love or some fictive kinship in a nonspecific human community alone doesn't seem to be sufficient. Such love and connectedness has to be materialised and incarnated in our actual lives. I certainly feel the insufficiency. Considering all this reexamination, I hope you do not see my desire for family involvement in marriage as a volte-face.

Now, as I face the prospects of entertaining a marriage arrangement, I am pondering anew on old understandings. It appears that I have some cultural privileges yet: this sense of community/social cohesion provided by common descent, shared cultural narrative and memory—all so life-giving for me who is part of a diaspora in this late twentieth century. I can see the value of this social system; it is the absence of choice in it that rankles me. But even on the matter of choice, I might be in a stronger position than I once was. I can always say no and live with the implications of that (which I haven't very well as you know), or I can always take a divorce in the event of a disastrous marriage relationship. Of course I will have to live with the pain I bring my parents. More importantly, I will have to live with my own pain. I suppose it is the thought that I will do my mortal best even at my own total expense that leads me to deem it best that I not see you or be in touch with the Vanderpols again. For I will be determined to give love a chance to blossom, even if it means abandoning my recent past in the West. Ah, but that's crazy! That cannot be love in any form, can it?

As I think about it, Margaret, perhaps it is not marriage that I fear (all things being equal, i.e., I have my say, etc.), but it is my future in a new relationship that I fear. It is the fear of the unfamiliar. Perhaps I am right to fear, as all should. For what are the guarantees in any relationship? My married friends tell me that it is no different than jumping into a cold pool. You get acclimatised. But will I get acclimatised to lacklustre living and giving? I am still thinking.

I realise that this is all too different on your side. You all seem to know a lot more about the other person before you marry than you do afterwards! Consider the comment, "He/she is not the person I married." Such familiarity before marriage brings with it its own expectations and illusions. In the Indian system we move into marriage with little expectation.

But let me be specific. I know you will be impatient with all these abstractions knowing that there is a story to tell at my end here. I got home. My parents were there to meet me at the airport. They were delighted to see me. Age has my mother in its tight and nasty grip. On the way home I learnt that my two-and-a-half prospects have been reduced to one—this reduction being both a relief and an added pressure, as all the energies are focused on the one egg. The candidate under consideration is the doctor chap suggested to me by my relatives in the States. The Indian postal and telegraph services, I am sure, have been working overtime these days. The communiqués between the two families are frequent and frenetic. Both are very eager and self-complimentary (leave my mother to her literary license!). I am without blemish, it would appear, and so is he. His family is of excellent social standing, tracing their roots back to ancient history and so on. He is tall, impressive, of the right age, accomplished, etc., etc. Memories of the old days are flashing back. The panic that I am getting lost in all this wheeling and dealing (and perhaps he as well) is setting in.

"Adjustment" is a word with some cachet at the time of meeting with prospective partners. It is a word which I have come to loathe and fear. The subtext for the ones who use it is that one sets aside one's standards and prior commitments, and to use a modern colloquialism, "gets real." For me it means the displacement of one's self to the point of alienation from one's self. Relatives and friends use it to cajole and coerce me into serious consideration of the chap on hand. And they all think that my interpretation of the word is exaggerated. My mother's favourite adjective for me is "adamant," and she is certain that my adamancy will destroy me (and her of course). I think that it will be my liberation!

In the present matter, I have decided to exercise some prerogatives on the basis of my age and experience. With the confidence that I am no longer some "innocent abroad," I have put my foot down and insisted to my parents that if they were to accompany me to "view"/"interview" this gent, they were sure to spoil the show. Since he does not have any immediate family members in Bangalore, where he works, I thought it was to my advantage to visit him there. There would be no nosy parties interested in steering this occasion. This in itself is a radical departure in tradition. Usually it is the male and family who come to the girl's family. That is the proper procedure. Girl going to meet boy is unheard of. While I have no intention of violating the sentiments behind the system, I am also aware from past experiences how fraught with misunderstandings and pressures it becomes when so many people are involved in contriving the occasion. My hangovers from these times were so damaging. I let my parents know that their accompaniment of me would destroy all possibility, as they can't help but dictate my dress, gait, speech and so on. It will all soon turn to puppetry. I realise also that my parents' pride and reputation are at stake. This whole idea of sending a girl off alone in pursuit of a man would, a few years ago, have been preposterous, but now I suppose a little flexibility for a lifelong goal was probably worth the risk from their standpoint. To be honest, while there is some excitement in the anticipation (not unlike your gambler analogy), it is the aftermath of this whole affair that I can do without. It eats away at your own sense of self (sound familiar?).

So, my friend, that's where I am at. The plan is to go over to Bangalore for two days and see him while I am there. I am using this opportunity to stay with an old college mate of mine. So the trip won't be a complete waste, I hope. I *know* and *feel* your presence. I wish that I could have you in my pockets these coming days. I miss you. I am sending this to Scotland, assuming that you will get it on your return from France.

Love,
Ivy

Take Care!

Dear Ivy,

Your first letter made it to Montpellier the day before I left; your second arrived here in Scotland this morning. After that memorable evening at the Vanderpols' home in Amsterdam, what with all your talk of leaving behind your life in the West forever, I was immensely relieved to receive your first letter! Not just because I would be incredibly sad if we lost touch, but also because I was fearful for your state of mind.

At one level, I can understand your sense of near despair and why you feel driven to consider such extremities as giving up totally on your life in the West: you have, in a sense, come to the end of the American dream—Ph.D., job, tenure, house, all now achieved-—and for what, and now what? I don't see your willingness to contemplate an arranged marriage at this stage as an about-turn at all. Ever since I have known you, I have been aware that for you the Western way of courtship was never really an option. I know that you have had the odd meeting set up for you with American men by kindly friends, but equally I have realised that the chasms between you were too great, the assumptions too different. What works as a creative dissonance between you and me in friendship would no doubt turn into a source of frustration and pain, even supposing you ever found a male Westerner with as much in common as you and I have.

I remember the first time I was in your house and I heard you speak your native language on the telephone to an Indian friend. I had already known you for over a year and felt that I knew you quite well. Suddenly, hearing you communicate in a tongue to which I had no access, shocked me into realising that there were whole worlds which were important to you of which I had not, and could not, have any part. Yet this is not true in reverse. One of the remarkable things about our friendship is that I feel you have entered into so many of my significant worlds, been introduced to so many of the people who mean the most to me. I have some sense of how important it might be for you to marry someone who speaks your own language, who shares so many of the small things about your culture that a Westerner, however sympathetic, never could.

And I am not even against the idea of arranged marriage as such. After all, despite all the fears of your loss of freedom and individuality you describe in telling of your flight from India, you have also clearly conveyed your sense of disappointment at the way in which Westerners make a god of freedom, and yet this very freedom is shot through with compulsion. Your present review of your various options, your experiences of both East and West, are probably inevitable and potentially very good.

My only worry is that your motivation will be one of fatalism and despair. I know how tired you are from all your struggling over many, many years, always feeling as if you are the one swimming against the tide. I also accept some of your questions now about the possible fundamental egotism of such a bucking of the system: what makes *you* so much more important than all your sisters? And yet, for whatever reason of combination of fate and inheritance and genes and upbringing and experience, you are who you are. It cannot be right to violate that, can it? By all means, be willing to consider a marriage that takes seriously all that your culture stands for: family and community obligations, the decision to learn to love rather than the insistence that one falls into love. All these are worthy values. But surely not at the expense of all those other strands of your identity: your independence, your passion, your intensity. Must a marriage be lacklustre? Does it have to be akin to jumping into a cold pool, knowing that one will eventually acclimatise? But one can also die of hypothermia!

Meantime, I am enjoying a couple of weeks back in Scotland with my folks. Such visits always make me think more about roots and identity. I wonder if my fierce attachment to the place is because I was a stranger here until my teenage years. The idea of home, then, is one I cannot take for granted as those with the confidence of having known a place intimately since babyhood can do. My mother and I took a picnic out to the hills above Loch Ness, where she spent her girlhood. Being among these ancient hills is always so peaceful, somehow, and I was struck again by their austere beauty. It's a landscape remote and lonely in its saturated tussocky green that is more moss than grass. But it is so reassuringly permanent. It's easy to believe that this is the oldest landscape in the world, with the easy rhythm of its hills, made gentle from millennia of weathering and smoothed into restfulness through long ages of endurance. There is, after all, not so very much more that could be worn away; the rounded rock black beneath the cropped green, all evidence that the elements and the elemental are, in these parts, already well acquainted. But I'm getting carried away: the combination of melancholic Scot and failed novelist is fatal!

What I'm trying to say is that I'm very sympathetic toward your desire to reconnect with your roots, but there's no undoing the last twenty years of your life either. So, Ivy, take care as you meet this doctor chap. I'm glad that you have insisted that the meeting will take place in circumstances that you feel comfortable with. That at least reassures me that you haven't totally relinquished the old spark of feistiness. And promise me that you will not simply drop contact with me and your other friends of recent years. That, too, would indicate an effort to adjust that would strike me as perverse.

I eagerly await your next letter with its news of The Meeting. I am nervous and excited on your behalf, so please write me as soon as you get back from Bangalore! Take with you the Taizé cross, and remember that you are in my prayers.

Much Love,
M.

The Meeting

Madras: August 15th, 1989

My dear Margaret:

My writing hands have been paralysed mainly because of a certain lethargy and indifference that I have surrendered to. It is hard to explain. To put it simply—the time, place and people here displace me out of my element, and I have in the last several days capitulated to the belief that in the very long run all is destiny and not much can be done by humans to alter one's course. While all my life I have tried to duck and cheat fate, I feel that the chase is now ended. Thus it is that I feel as if I have suspended all sense of propriety and proportion—losing control rather than taking control. Such free association this—let me try to be a little more specific for your sake.

I am back from Bangalore. Where shall I begin? The beginning lies in the end. Perhaps not. I wish you were here with me and that my mind was some sort of glass container that you could see through. Explaining/describing takes so much energy right now. I'll try to tell you all, chronologically.

I left Madras on August 9th with the prayers and blessings of my parents. Now there is humour here—you see, my mother picked out my wardrobe to assure "attractiveness." I promised her that I would oblige her request. Of course, the irony is that the whole assemblage ensured "unattractiveness" in my opinion. The clothes were dated from the standpoint of Indian fashion. She wanted me to wear certain kinds of jewelery, certain colours, etc., etc. Personally, I would be turned off by men who were turned on by such distaste. But then I wasn't up for a row. Did my mum know how self-defeating her dictates might become? Secretly I thought that this would in its own way be a test of the man. Would he look *at* me or would he see *me*? In any case I let Mummy have her way, as in the end I hoped that it would turn out in my favour (he wouldn't be interested). I promised them that I would "behave," i.e., not engage in the proverbial religious/political discussions that would embarrass them. No doubt I was angry, thinking that they still found me so malleable. They wanted me to call them if the meeting turned out to be positive; if not—well, I wasn't given an alternative suggestion. I promised to keep my promises. Thus I left.

I received your postcard from Taizé and I held tenaciously to your inscription of Mary's response: "Behold the handmaiden of the Lord; be it unto me according to thy word." These days I have felt quite desolate and despondent as I think of my future as a married woman. In my prayers, I reminded God of my earlier petition—of my desire for someone to love, of my need for worship and celebration in partnership. Frequently, I have referred to our friendship and pleaded that I have such a friendship in marriage. Perhaps this is all the wrong way of praying, for beneath these prayers I sense a real resistance to move beyond the familiar—and thus my dictation to God. But I do not know any better (which is really what the present crisis is all about—fear and ignorance). This was my state when I arrived in Bangalore.

There was a joker in the pack. In Bangalore, I was to stay at the home of a friend of mine. I have known Gita since I was five. It was from here that I was to set out to meet "Abraham," the fellow in question. She is married to a renowned scientist, and they have a nine-year-old son. Hers was a love- (meaning she met him on her own) cum-arranged marriage (the parents got involved to give the semblance of propriety, consent, etc.). A short while into marriage she started to become deeply unhappy. Their dissatisfaction was out in the open, and I felt like an unwitting hostage to their misfortunes. She was threatening to leave the marriage. What was I to do? Be a referee in this situation, chuck up my plans for glorious matrimony or what? I was in a quandary psychologically and emotionally.

No doubt, these were inauspicious environs to leave for a potentially auspicious meeting. I thought of those families who consulted the astrologers to arrange the proper time, place and suchlike for these weighty meetings. If only my parents knew where I had located myself to launch myself from! But then they would be quick to remind me that things were a mess because Gita took her life into her own hands by choosing this man against her parents' wishes in the first place. While they may have a point, I was moved by the pain in this home, especially by the forlorn face of the dear little nine-year-old boy. I downplayed the subject of my impending meeting. My friend had told me quite directly that she envied my single life and would not recommend marriage to anyone! I didn't know what to do with such confirmation.

On August 12th I said good-bye to Gita, who waved pensively as I took off in an auto-rickshaw to meet Abraham at his aunt's home. Gita's marital situation swayed my mood considerably. I had been badly shaken by my stay there and was quite undone by its impact on the forthcoming meeting. Dwell on all things lovely and true—right! I was pessimistic and felt a sense of detachment as I traveled to keep this ominous tryst.

I arrived on time (pretty impressive for me, don't you think? But then when my parents are involved I try to get it right). I was met by an urbane, well-preserved woman at the door. She was the aunt, of course. She beckoned me inside to the drawing room. And then…and then I turned to set eyes on the man himself. My editorial senses kicked in. I was most unimpressed. My heart sank. He looked exhausted. Tired eyes, shrunken socks, frayed collar, terribly *plain*. I was of course dressed at my mother's behest. No, no, this was not the man for me. There was no "energy" between us at all. Everything thereafter seemed largely irrelevant.

His aunt was very gracious. She served us tea and was keen to make me most comfortable. She and her husband had been students in the U.S. in the 1940s and told me about their days there, etc. A little later Abraham suggested that we go out to a park and chat in private for a bit. I was open to the idea but I thought it was pointless since I had already made up my mind. Since my parents expected a blow by blow narration of "what he said and what I said," I decided I would oblige him. I was a little disconcerted, as this was the first time I was going to be alone with him. Fortunately it was still early in the evening, and I calculated that if I was to be in any untoward situation, I would just hail a taxi and return to confirm my friend's gloomy perspective about the male species. Well, Margaret, we got out to a lakeside park in the city and went to a little restaurant.

Abraham did most of the talking. I was concentrating on being "sweet and subservient." I answered his questions about my work, my life in the U.S., etc. It was very clear that there was no future when he took out his cigarette. You know of my allergies to cigarette smoke. Well, we spent about three hours engaging in small talk, and as night fell I suggested that it was time to conclude, as Gita would be up waiting. While he did not give me any great offense, I was clearly not "turned on." At the end of the meeting he asked me if I would like to meet him for lunch the next day. I relented. Yes, the looming faces of my parents again!

In many ways I did not look forward to returning to Gita's.

On my way there I decided to be fairly circumspect with the details of my meeting, as I had to conduct a postmortem of the evening for myself. I shared briefly but kept my counsel. That night I prayed for strength to be truly kind and patient in my manner with this man the next day. You know this about me. I am so easily bored and wanting to get on with it. A terrible streak! I was also struggling since I saw once more the denouement of a grand mission that had been many months and prayers in the works.

In any case I went the next day, a Sunday, and met him at the appointed place for lunch. He had been to church and then had come on to meet me. He suggested a wonderful restaurant that served authentic South Indian foods from all the various provinces including Kerala, a rarity on the gourmet's charts! Kerala, the southwest Indian state, is of course the native land of both our ancestors, and it is that shared feature that forms the entire basis for this meeting—shared lineage, language, food, religious traditions, etc., ensue from this shared geography.

Early on I decided that I had to be true to myself and true to this poor man and stop this charade, this false "behaving" and start with some integrity and "misbehave" if you know what I mean (in my former mode I am sure that I would have appeared as a stranger to you). If he took offense, that in itself would be revealing, wouldn't it? For a start I asked why he had been to church that morning. He started to tell me about his belief in God. Very modest, no sophisticated theology worked out. This then led me to ask quite naturally why he chose medicine. Partly fascinated by the field, partly in memory of his grandfather, who had also been a doctor, he said. Into our conversation I began to get the sense that this man was mature and decent enough not to misinterpret me to his family. I started to feel safe with him. We started to talk about other things quite freely—women's issues in India, liberation theology, questions of social justice and so on. In fact he had brought along a booklet arguing for the abolition of dowry to give to me. He wanted me to know the current debate on the matter in India. I did not misconstrue this gesture, and think that he was merely trying to impress me with his own progressive view towards women and so on.

After the meal, he asked if I was interested in going to an art museum with him. I agreed. There was an art exhibit on Hindu art. I was impressed at how well-versed he was in Hindu mythology. He sounded like a Hindu priest, but he shrugged my comments of amazement off by saying that his father had been a professor in Indian philosophy, and thus his own knowledge of Hinduism was really quite unremarkable. This dimension in a man, in any man, i.e., an inherent consciousness of and contentment in his Indianness was of vital importance to me. It is a journey I am on myself.

The afternoon went on with informative exchanges. He told me of his readings of Athol Fugard's plays. Margaret, you know that not a soul in this world can keep me down on the phenomenal Fugard. Any mention of Fugard would have me flying into a paroxysm of ecstasy. In even this I desisted. Instead, I appeared quite nonchalant, making some passing mention of having read a few myself. Inside I was struggling to keep my amazement that anyone in this country would be interested in a South African playwright, never mind this haggard looking doctor. He is presently reading one of Ann Oakley's works, which was yet another startler.

You see, Margaret, I had "matched" quite closely with many suitors in terms of my interests and hobbies previously. So I wasn't going to be overimpressed this time. Abraham must have picked up my continuing lack of fire. He also seemed well aware of the pressures at my home front without my having to tell him. He has a sister, you see. As he was strategising my response for the next few days, I explained myself by saying that I was one who took a mighty long time deciding to even buy a saree. Often I would go from shop to shop and return home with nothing. Of course, in so doing I did know rather quickly what I did not want. Surely making up my mind about a life partner would take a heck of a lot more time, I said. His response to my analogy took me back. He said that he was content with a couple of shirts from any shop at all. He himself was not all that fastidious. I am still processing what that means. On the one hand he confirmed what I was thinking about him, i.e., his simplicity. On the other I had to rethink my own nature. Am I too fussy, too demanding? In any case, he said that he would spare me any embattlements by suggesting that I tell my parents that he needed more time to think about this proposition, and thus it was best for us to write each other for a few months before we could come to any definitive conclusions on further direction. This was August. He suggested that we could take until November to decide one way or the other. I was delighted at the reprieve from him and my parents. This could have a noble ending after all! We thanked each other, got each other's address and took leave.

While the content of the meeting itself was no different from all my previous ones, what of course was vastly improved was the process itself. There was a great deal more space when we were left together as adults to our own judgments. I spent eleven hours in all, far more than with any of my previous suitors, and most of the time we were unattended. I suspect that I saw a bit of the real Abraham, although I have no way of knowing enough to have an adequate sense of him. I do know that I was "performing" for him and for my family's sake, and I did not declare my hand completely. But what could I have done differently? In the absence of "physics" or "chemistry," I just did not have the energy. How am I going to explain this?

To conclude, Abraham is in many ways quite acceptable (faith, intellect, social awareness, etc.); on the other hand my *heart* has not responded to him, and I am concerned about that. I am just not drawn to him. The civil war renting me apart leads me to acknowledge how irrevocably westernised I have become. I am also waging a war with God. For so long I wanted an Indian man who shared my cultural Memory and basic values, and now when one is brought, I resist.

Margaret, I must send this, as otherwise it will take another day to post it. I got home yesterday. I have recounted everything to my parents. Much to my surprise they have been enormously supportive. I hope it will last. It must be both our ages—this mellowing. God has been good on that front. On the other hand it is that much harder now that I have to execute or dismiss this case on my own—the burden of choice really. Please pray for direction. My dear sister-in-law is a helpful presence. I so wish you were here.

Love,
Ivy

"She Protesteth Too Much"

Scotland: August 30, 1989

Dear Ivy,

Never have I been so eager to read a letter when it came through the letter box! It so happened that the postman arrived just as my mother and I were about to drive off to visit a small dress shop in a village a few miles away. I whipped your letter from the carpet in the hall and took it along in case I found an opportunity to read it. Never has my perusal of potential dresses on a shopping trip been so cursory! Whilst my mother tried on various outfits, slightly bemused at my uncustomary disinterest, I stood transfixed in the middle of the shop, devouring your letter.

A meeting described at such length and in such detail! It must be significant! Ivy, I quickly detected that you are seriously interested in this smoking, tired-looking doctor who doesn't care about what shirt he wears. Normally, when you meet potential suitors—at least since I have known you—you are very quick to sort them out and dismiss them. I well remember the night that one came to visit you in Boston. Although he looked good on paper, you figured out within five minutes of meeting that this was not the man for you. I remember you telling me later of how you tried to get through the meal as quickly as possible, dispatched the suitor to the spare room pleading exhaustion and a headache, and then phoned me. Poor Mr. Wrong was equally speedily dispatched from our conversation, two minutes or so, no longer.

But not so with Mr. Abraham. Ivy, I was fascinated by your account. I am far from convinced with your analogy of buying a saree—unless that was a way of being kind to the man by not rejecting him outright. In my shopping trips with you, especially when it came to buying clothes for me, you have always been anything but indecisive, and even rather impulsive! And in your previous encounters with potential husbands, I have been struck by how quickly you seemed able to reach a decision, dismiss the poor man and put the whole experience behind you.

As I read you now, it seems to me that there are two warring impulses within you. On the one hand, you want to continue just as you are and respond to this next suitor in your path just as you have done with so many of the other men you have met. You are rightly reluctant to give up your independence, and no doubt at least a part of you is keen to prove, given how long the battle has been (and how stubborn you can be), that yet again, someone of your family's choosing could not possibly be the man for you. Yet, "she protesteth too much," I thought as you recounted how you agreed to meet him the next day for lunch, allegedly to please your parents. Since when have you taken such pains? It is obvious that, despite your resistance, this man has many of the qualities you need and admire. Don't dismiss him too easily!

But I am being presumptuous here. You are still undecided and, as you say, there is a great deal at stake. Not every man could take your independence and strength of character. And could either one of you seriously consider giving up your world to be with the other? One of you would have to forsake a very great deal. There are so many momentous questions to ponder, and even though this man has generously given you a way out and you do not have to make up your mind until November, that is only a matter of months. Such a decision would be considered most hasty here in the West. Can't you see him again— arrange a holiday for him in the States or something?

At any rate, my earlier fears are somewhat assuaged. I no longer think you are at risk of making a hasty decision based on exhaustion and despair. You sound in your right mind once again, and I am convinced that, either way, you will make a good choice. I feel for you in the heavy burden of this decision. Do you know what he is really thinking? Is he keen on you (or whatever the appropriate term is over there)? It would be ironic and really disappointing if you were drawn to a man for the first time and he showed no interest in return. But he sounds like a kind person who would not toy with your feelings. He'd better not!

Ivy, my thoughts continue with you in your last days in India. I very much hope that your parents continue to be supportive and give you the space you need to make an authentic decision. Are you in touch with him meantime? What does you sister-in-law make of all this? Write again soon, telling me how your thoughts are progressing.

Much Love,
M.

Visitation on the Night Train

Madras: September 7th, 1989

Dear Margaret,

Thank you for your posthaste reply. Your words are my lifeline just now! You have detected in my previous letter some currents that I am myself not in touch with. Why, if I am not interested, have I belaboured my descriptions of Abraham with you? I think that my details to you were merely in sequence with my giving account to my parents as to why I had chosen to reject Abraham.

But there's something else here, Margaret. Something that I haven't had the courage to share with anyone, not even with you, for fear of the implications. It has to do with a rather incredible experience that I had on the train back to Madras. You see, I took a night train back. It was a strange night. As that slow train rumbled its way through the sleeping villages, I lay awake, fighting for my future. The experience for me was of biblical proportions—as if I had been visited by the great God of the universe. I am hesitant to write about it not only because of its intimate nature but because of its strangeness. But I must share it with you for my own sanity's sake. It was unlike anything else. There was something disturbing and miraculous about it, and I have been haunted by it. Well here's how it was.

As you might imagine, I boarded the train and retired for the night with only one thing on my mind. How the heck was I going to avoid yet another altercation with my family? What was I going to say without doing injury to this poor man? Clearly they knew the outcome by now, as I had not rung them as promised. It was the defense of the decision that had to be thought through this night. Oddly I was not permitted this privilege. Instead, I had a sort of mystical "visitation" experience, shall I say, wherein I was badgered with a list. A list of unconditional prerequisites in a marriage I desired. Since I had been a twenty-year veteran at this, it was no problem drafting one. A man of faith. A man who loves the world. A man who could love me. A man I could respect. A man who could respect me. A man who was acquainted with grief (this was especially important to me for all sorts of reasons). A man who was humble, and so on. But there was one feature that had become so second nature to me that it had never been subjected to any great examination; it was just assumed—*I had to be turned on by this man.* Well, this night this list kept being thrust before me rather persistently. I was unwilling to engage, as I was well aware that the night was passing and I had better come up with something reasonable to tell my parents early the next morning. Further, this whole experience was odd because in the past I had no problem at all putting the subject of my meeting behind me.

I felt that I was being held to account by some strange Spirit, a kind and good Spirit it was. Abraham was brought back to me. Well, as I told you there was no way I could consider Abraham seriously because of the lack of "energy" between us. It was a recipe for disaster to pursue someone who did not hold your attention. Well, Margaret, I felt compelled in this time of nocturnal encounter to define "energy," "being turned on," and I was terribly unnerved as I backed into a corner unable to define it as anything other than lust. The concept of "being turned on" I knew, but the conception itself (the actuality of "chemistry," "being in love," and so on) escaped my grasp. I was humiliated and embarrassed by my cockiness and utter folly. I was unwilling for this revolution at this stage in my life. I needed no more lessons. No, no, no—not him, never. He was without flash and flamboyance. It would be a loveless life!

I was challenged back into the ring. He was a man of quiet faith, was he not? As the son of a political activist, philosopher and lover of literature and the grandson of a doctor, Abraham had inherited all the right sympathies for a meaningful life. Has humility ever resided happily with flamboyance? He wasn't overly impressed with me; is this not what I wanted? He was the oldest in his family, and after the death of his parents he saw to the education and marriages of his younger siblings; did such caring and provision not appeal to my sensibilities on love and suffering?

I could go on engaging you rhetorically, Margaret. The important thing was that I was haunted by something I thought I had settled much earlier. I was finding out that I was infected by the irrational bug of romance more viscerally than I had thought. In one night, the fine silk of my illusions started to unravel. I was not only forced to see my one demon full in the face; I experienced something worse. Some strange power left my being, and as I proceeded to retrieve it, I was led inevitably back to the person of Abraham. What can I say? Do you see why I am reluctant to share this without very great caution? Time alone will tell of the sense or the "non-sense" of what I am telling you. I was terrified at facing my parents. I decided to shelve my strange encounter with the night. I tried to gather up my resources for the next day. I was sure that I was bringing a cyclone in my trail. But then the tides turned. My parents were quite complaisant with my choice to postpone a decision. The expected battles had come to naught.

So now you can see that I am wrestling with two realities—the public and sensible one, and the private and surreal one.

The train episode I dare not tell anyone for fear of misappropriation. Yet, on the other hand, I, who see myself as having paid heed all along to the possibility of goodness, cannot disregard the experience. If there is a God and if there is such a thing called faith on earth, I feel that the two met on that train, and I have been stopped in my tracks.

No doubt I am thinking a lot about this "chemistry" stuff. I am not even sure that it is altogether Western, as it is the universal tendency in human beings to engage anarchically in the absence of social strictures. This is what I see in the West—uninhibited social intercourse between men and women (I am aware that it wasn't always this way). This is what I was drawn to in the romantic fiction of the *grande dames*. Now I am trying to see how it all fits in a particular context with a particular person, keeping in mind what it is that is of importance to me while drawing on the strengths of the East. I feel like I am trapped in a crisis of meaning/confidence of sorts—not knowing where to turn.

I trust that you will continue to pray for me. My sister-in-law is very good to confer with. I fear an uncertain future, fear making mistakes. Fear is part of my daily mood. Either way, I am on the verge of a major decision in the next few months. In the meanwhile, like Mary the mother of Jesus, I am pondering the visitation on the night train. What do you say? I am frightened hourly.

My love to your parents. Enjoy your holiday. Thanks for all your understanding.

Love,
Ivy

The Stuff of Our Attractions

England: September 15th, 1989

Dear Ivy,

Many thanks for your last letter. I feel privileged to be taken into your confidence in a matter so personal, so momentous and so difficult to understand, and I can well appreciate your reluctance to put it all into words. There is the danger, if one talks or even writes too early about a thing, that one is thereby making it more of a possibility, a reality in one's mind. And in a matter so delicate, where the discernment leads you into such unfamiliar territory, it is vital that you have time to ponder all these things on your own and give time and space for the meanings to gradually emerge as they will.

I have been thinking a lot about your account of the train journey back to Madras. I tried to picture you there in that train compartment, wrestling through the night. As I said in my last letter, such indecision is, I think, uncharacteristic for you. I tend to think of you as a decisive, even impulsive person, so your inability to put the whole experience quickly behind you is unusual. This man sounds like the first serious contender in all the scores of suitors you have met so far!

Your comments on "energy" and "being turned on" also gave me pause for thought. You are right, that although you and I may *think* we are looking for qualities a little more lofty, how much of our attraction to men is reducible to simple lust? I have known for a while that you are drawn to the dashing, glamorous type, the Richard Burtons of this world. No doubt, as you suggest, this is a part of your Mills and Boon inheritance that has lingered even at a subconscious level. Even when we think we have deconstructed Romantic Love, its vestiges remain so potent!

So, Abraham is very different from this type, and you wonder if you can relinquish your love of flash and flamboyance? Isn't one colourful, dynamic character plenty in a partnership? His qualities sound immensely attractive in the more profound sense of our "deep-souled desires" that I was talking of some letters ago. I know that I don't need to tell you to consider this man very carefully. Continue to weigh up your experiences on your homeward journey in that train carriage in the Indian night. It sounds as if there is so much in this Abraham that is potentially compatible with your best self. It may not even be a case of admitting you cannot have it all, the glamour as well as the humility, and therefore settling for the bird in the hand. Maybe the two are incompatible in any case, and the choice before you now is about giving up the last vestiges of your Romantic Dream for what that deeper journey in you has been preparing you for.

I look anxiously for your next letter, no doubt when you are back in the States. I think it will be good for you to return to your life in the West and reconsider all the events of recent weeks from the very different perspective over there.

Love,
M.

Waiting

Boston: September 17th, 1989

Dear Margaret:

I am on the other side of the Atlantic now. I am really looking forward to talking with you soon.

It was hard leaving my parents the way I did. I know that in their heart of hearts they long for me to say "Yes" to Abraham. But I cannot. I've held out too long to cave in now.

I would like to update you on my last days in India and since. A few days after I returned from Bangalore, I wrote a note to Abraham to thank him for his time with me when I was there. He wrote back saying that he was glad to have met me and that even if nothing was to transpire between us, he hoped that I would call him up whenever I was in Bangalore next.

Since you are on holiday and incommunicado, I called up my cousin in New York to consult with him on Abraham. He, like you, suggests that I meet him at least once before I say yea or nay. While the idea is good, I don't think it is feasible considering the financial cost and also the implications of keeping this meeting private without pressure from family. He was kind enough to offer me the fare, reminding me of the seriousness of the matter. I in the meanwhile have another idea in mind, which is to write the longest letter possible and reveal my real identity to Abraham. I cannot see any sense in masquerading at this point. In light of the night on the train, I have to give God, Abraham and myself my very best shot on this affair. My cousin supports the idea (his wife doesn't, fearing that I might scare Abraham away), so I think I will follow through. Besides, time is not on my side, and this is a risk worth taking.

Later that day:

Margaret, my jet lag helped me stay up odd hours at my computer. I compiled an eight-page letter to Abraham. I presented myself as exhaustively as I could, with all the integrity I could muster. I told him really about all the seamy sides to me. By seamy I meant all those aspects that traditional men might find difficult to tolerate in a woman like myself—independence, my various friendships, my hope for complete mutuality in a marriage and so on. I wonder what Abraham will think. His reply will tell all.

Two weeks later:

I haven't heard from him yet. It was good to talk with you after all these weeks. I am beginning to wonder. I have to be away in Germany for the next two weeks, and if I don't hear from Abraham by then it will be a clear indication of his lack of interest. I still expect from him a brief acknowledgment of my letter out of basic decency though. I don't like this uncertainty, this feeling of being put on hold.

The semester is about to start and things are again getting busy at my end. I am looking forward to visiting Berlin so soon after the fall of the wall. I'll send you a postcard.

Love,
Ivy

Keeping Close Counsel

England: October 7th, 1989

Dear Ivy,

    I'm concerned by Abraham's silence. What's he playing at? I thought he was sympathetic, even favourable. Do you think he has had second thoughts?

    In any case, I do not think you were wrong to send him that long letter introducing yourself. It's important that he has some idea of what he would be letting himself in for with you, and if he can't stomach it, then he's not the man for you! Still, it must be hard for you, feeling as if your life continues to hang in the balance.

    Are many of your friends over there aware of what is going on? I could imagine it is quite hard if you are having to explain yourself in all this. I happened to mention your circumstances to one of my friends here—Julie, do you remember her? She came to dinner while you were visiting. Her response was no doubt exactly what mine would have been a few years ago. She was asking how you were, and when I absent-mindedly mentioned that you were trying to decide whether or not to marry, she expressed amazement that you would have any truck with the arranged-marriage system. As I leapt to its defense, I realised that I had come a long way! But I also felt the kind of weariness that you must feel on countless occasions when called to be the interpreter, the defender of your culture to people who are starting from such a different set of premises. I found I really didn't want to enter into the discussion. I hope you are not finding such pressure to explain yourself an added burden at a time when you no doubt need as much energy as you can muster to focus elsewhere.

Meantime, I have returned south after a refreshing time in Scotland. My energies are renewed and my perspectives refreshed…which is just as well, with a new academic year all but upon us! I am teaching two courses this year, one on contemporary British fiction, the other on postcolonial literature. It will be a lot of hard work, what with all the college responsibilities too, but no doubt this will help to keep me focused and out of mischief! (No unattached visiting academics on the horizon, thankfully!) Seriously, I am really looking forward to the teaching. Thinking through so many of the issues that both courses will raise with a group of bright undergraduates will be immensely stimulating.

Ivy, I do hope you hear soon, one way or the other. Keep me posted! I look forward to the next installment.

Much love,
M.

Courtship Redefined

Boston: October 15th, 1989

Dear Margaret:

Thanks a lot for that understanding letter. Since our time on the phone is so expensive, we'll still have to rely on the post for our extended thoughts.

As I told you the other day, I was quite disappointed at not having a reply from Abraham on my return from Germany. My disappointment is not so much an indication of any feelings I might have towards him other than that I am sorry at my wasted effort and feel a little exposed after having written that long epistle. I hardly know the man to say that I trust him with its contents.

As I have been dealing with the silence from the other side, I was talking with my friend Lila, and at some point she asked me point blank if I would miss Abraham if I never heard from him again. As I thought about it, I replied that yes, I would be slightly sad at an aborted possibility. She was quick to remind me that that was sufficient indication of the embryonic development of affection for this man. While I found that a helpful insight, I will not be swayed by such measures and subtle pressures. You are absolutely right—it is very difficult to discuss this subject with anyone at all around here. It takes too much explaining and turns out to be quite pointless. Most people's premises are nonstarters for me. In that sense I feel that the train episode continues to frame my thinking. I'll explain what I mean in a bit.

Yesterday I called home to find out if they had heard anything positive or negative by way of Abraham and party. My mother said that she was so glad I called because she had just had a call from Abraham wondering if I had received his letter, and why I had not replied. She then went on to tell me that there had been a postal strike some weeks back. This explains the silence. She said that she would convey my enquiry and would suggest to him that he write again.

Getting back to my earlier reference to my experience on the train, what I mean is that I've had to answer two repeated questions in the last several weeks. Why not see him again, considering that November is not that far away? Are you in love? Both for me are culturally loaded questions, and I am never able to explain myself satisfactorily to either question.

These repeated queries take us into the territory of courtship. What is acceptable and what are the values at stake? I'll address the first question (I'll take the second one up in my next) of seeing him again due to the shortness of time between now and October. Firstly, as I think about it, I wonder what good will come out of *seeing* him again? In other words what will I accomplish this time that I didn't the last time? I find letters more useful in this regard, especially in these early stages of acquaintance, because I am able to be more measured and deliberate about what I say, rather than getting all excited and impetuous as I am prone to among friends or being as wooden as I was in Bangalore.

Secondly, and significantly, is my concern about being alone with him or any man for such purposes. You know well that when I am intensely engaged in conversation with someone I get beside myself. In no time I am tugging away at their hands or sleeves to make my point. What do you think will be the impact of such behaviour when I know that I am engaging with a man I might potentially marry? While open display of physical affection is seen as a mark of love and troth in the West, the opposite is the case in the East. Such public expressions of affection are seen as vulgar and disrespectful. I remember clearly how when I was walking with Abraham in Bangalore, I tripped and just about fell into a huge gaping manhole. I pulled myself back, nervous that Abraham would have to come to my help. If he had touched me in that instance, I would have felt a bit violated. I appreciated very much his not doing so. However, I am almost certain that had it been a crisis, he would have stepped in. The point I am trying to make is that the value of not touching the other until marriage is taken quite seriously.

After living in the West so long, I can see the importance of this value in my tradition when I see how many hands, lips, bodies and beds are shared before one chooses to marry. Surely such serial giving of oneself has an impact on so much of one's present and future being! I am not even trying to hold a discussion here on the pros and cons of physical involvement outside marriage; I am merely struck by the importance of abstinence that one practices out of respect and value for the self and other. Abstinence is also a statement of one's awareness of sexual potency in self and other. Especially for those interested in getting acquainted for the sake of marriage, abstinence from physical entanglements facilitates clearer procedure and freer departures, if you know what I mean. Little is lost when the body has abstained. No doubt this is clearly a cultural/subjective/personal stance, but I feel the validity of it. There is a certain freedom that comes from self-control.

There is also among some a sense of false dualism of sexual touch and nonsexual touch in courtship. Is there such a thing as nonsexual touch between heterosexual adults? If so, why do men and women in the West seek to touch each other rather than members of the same sex, unless it is an explicitly homosexual contact? Further, such touch is often exclusively among mates or potential mates. Prolonged and repeated patterns of touch and other physical interaction are indeed sexual, and it is false to suggest that sexual intercourse alone is sexual while all other forms of interaction are nonsexual.

The suggestion that mutual consent instead of social consent is sufficient does not quite pan out (but then of course there is the problem of the "social" being flawed as well). In that sense I am struck by my well-meaning friends' suggestions to go out with Abraham for a while and see if I "love" him. What do they mean by this "going" and "loving"? How far do you "go" and how do you "love"? Drawing the lines around sharing the bed, i.e., sleeping together, is a false marker. What about all the sexual socialising that goes on in the name of courtship that leads one quite naturally to the bed/altar when in fact these may be bad choices? I suppose I am really talking here about dating and mating as people in the West have come to take for granted.

When public display of affection through physical contact is a cultural imperative to dating in the West, where such affection is seen as being "in love," "spontaneous," "free," etc., there is also an attendant loss of control that goes with these exchanges. Frequently such sexual coziness colours the couple's perspective of their future. I see this social pattern in the West as a significant departure from that of the East and really from its own in an earlier time. While intimacy before marriage is a prelude to the sacrament in the West, in the East it is the postlude to marriage. In the latter I see more potential (no guarantees however) for commitment, value, respect and meaning. Particularly as a female, I feel the need keenly to be in control of my body. I do not want to squander it in the name of love and be faced with the task of retrieving the wreckage after any misguided investment in a man.

In my case, while I am naturally terrified at the prospect of "courting" long distance, I would not have done it any differently if he lived nearby (I hope so anyhow). I am operating with the assumption that regardless of how well one knows the other (statistics attest to this), the marriage still remains an incredibly risky endeavour. Knowing the pitfalls of "seeing" each other, I would opt for the Indian way of staying away from him until I am convinced that both of us are willing to commit ourselves to each other. The important thing for me is that I take responsibility for my choice of whom I marry, and that I be strongly supported by my immediate family and community, not only for their blessing but also as an insurance in the event of a tragedy. The rest is Grace. Grace alone. The Grace of God.

Don't get me wrong, Margaret. While our letters have often been a means of communicating with each other, they have also enabled the clarification for ourselves of many of our own positions that go largely unexamined. Our letters have certainly done that for me. Throughout, I have let you know of how fraught both our cultural systems are on the questions of intimacy. All I am saying here is that assuming all things are equal, i.e., two individuals have committed themselves mutually to pursue an acquaintance for the potential of marriage, I find the regulations that the Indian system places on the couple more helpful for all concerned. In case you think that I can afford this route because I am Indian, I'd like you to know that that is not necessarily the case. We can *all* negotiate with our cultures. It takes time, much reflection and moral strength. In this sense it is not finally an East-West thing.

I am reminded of a meeting I had last week with a Canadian

student. She told me that she wished so much that she could have an "arranged marriage." Somehow when people use that term in the West I pick up a certain glibness, a certain facility. I asked her what she meant. Did she wish that friends or family would undertake to suggest/bring a man to her *or* did she mean that she would be willing to alter radically her cultural assumptions on courtship and marriage? She admitted that she hadn't quite thought about it in terms of the latter, rather she was just not up to being a schemer and a hunter of men. She was tired.

In the first sense of "arranged," i.e., that the individual is "brought" to you, I see that all partnerships everywhere are "arranged" in varying degrees. While the arrangements seem to be less evident in the West, if you stop to examine it, instances of truly blind love are rare (if nonexistent). There are always some prearranged factors—social and economic status being key. These are broken down in terms of education, class, religion, region, income, race, etc., etc. More specifically, one hardly "picks" someone up on the street or on a train (although that does happen on occasion); more likely there is a church, workplace, dinner party at friends', college date and so on.

The unique feature about "arrangement" in India lies in the second part of my question to the student—the way in which communities orchestrate the nature of the relationship between the couple in question. The expectations of the couple from meeting to parting or from meeting to mating are clearly prescribed. To Westerners for whom the culture of romance and individual freedom reigns supreme, such social restrictions seem archaic and problematic. On the other hand, if one finds any value to such restraint in order that emotional, psychological and sexual violence is reduced between men and women, and if one sees that the sacramental value of sex and marriage might be restored, I am confident that *individual* men and women can negotiate alternative forms of "getting to know" and "getting to love," and who knows but that an alternative culture, an alternative freedom itself, is in the making!

Dear Margaret, this is way too long. I cannot believe that I have spent so much time telling you about why I do not feel the need to see Abraham, and I have hardly mentioned my trip to Germany. It was very good. I think my paper went well. I'll tell you more when we talk. I am so sorry that the summer is over for both of us and we will both be back to the grind. Your course on postcolonial literature sounds very interesting. Although, as we've discussed before, the concept of "postcolonial" is problematic in light of world affairs these days. I wish I were reading some of the material. I am sure you'll do a great job of it. I want to hear more. I will write again soon. Take care.

Love,
Ivy

INTERLUDE

I remember vividly that momentous summer, the summer of Ivy's courtship. Neither of us had really imagined that such a thing was ever going to happen. My impression was that long since, Ivy had given up on the serious possibility of marriage. She had come to accept, so I thought, that she would never fit into the institution as she saw it embodied in either East or West: either model of matrimony would be impossible for someone who was so dissatisfied with both. She was also aware of her own streak of perfectionism and often told me that she would not be a fit partner for marriage. I accepted this, although from time to time, I feared for her and wondered how she would continue to make her way in life, riven as she was between two cultures. Her position as cultural refugee seemed, from my perspective, to be growing increasingly painful.

So, when the drama of the summer and her courtship began to unfold, it was, for me, like following the plot of a compelling novel whose storyline was utterly new to me, and whose ending I could not guess. And yet, the implications for us both, of course, felt much more momentous than anything confined to the pages of fiction. So much of what we had shared and discussed was at stake. Was Ivy about to give it all up, betray our hopes for something better? In which case, I would not only have lost a priceless friendship, I would also have lost some important dreams along with her demise. But there was also the more hopeful possibility that my friend was actually forging a path which somehow carried the best of both our cultures, that she might be finding a way to embody in her life what we had both been reaching toward for so long: a better way of love that took account of our identities as individuals yet firmly rooted us in community. We were also determined that as individuals, we should not be diminished by marriage, but should take courage from the marriage relationship, and draw strength to serve God and the world more effectively than would be possible alone.

Ivy's letters after her meeting with Abraham gave me much food for thought. Faced with the real possibility of a viable relationship for the first time in her life, her thoughts about the relationship between a man and a woman with a view toward partnership in marriage took on flesh and bones in a way that had been previously impossible. Her thoughts about East-West values in matters of courtship were deeply challenging, and perhaps more than ever before, I was forced to look very hard at Western procedures and to see which of my inherited patterns I actually did value and which I found hard to defend in the light of my friend's observations and criticisms. It was also sometimes hard, seeing that some things were far from ideal, and yet knowing that one is one's culture to a large extent. One cannot simply abandon its meanings and habits at will. So behind these letters, Ivy's weighing and sifting was being echoed in my own thoughts. Whilst some of this was enlightening, some thoughts were simply unsettling.

Naturally, amidst all this, I was very concerned for my friend in her ordeal. I felt slightly helpless: she was operating in a world with which I was unfamiliar; my accumulated wisdom was simply inadequate for the choices and experiences she was encountering. And yet, I felt intimately connected in the whole process. If it all turned to dust, I knew I would grieve as if my own hopes had been dashed. If something precious was born, the promise of creating something new and fine would be my promise too. The stakes felt very high, and the waiting to see how it would all turn out felt long. . . .

PART FOUR

New Horizons

The Decision

Boston: October 30th, 1989

Dear Margaret:

Where were you when I needed you? I called several times last night. No luck. While I hope to talk with you well before this gets to you, I am writing to balance out the phone bill! Besides, so much has been happening that I realise that I have not written to you for a long time. My writing energies have been temporarily diverted!

As you know, the letters have been going back and forth

149

between myself and Abraham for some weeks now (interspersed with an occasional call). All very long letters of self-disclosure, but none of them have been "love letters." We have dealt with each other more as prospective roommates, telling the other of preferences and prejudices, exchanging views and so on. Overall the process has been very good. It is amazing how much we do have in common, although our personalities and our styles are diametrically different. I am learning a lot—unlearning really. The nocturnal visit on the train continues to reveal itself as a lodestar in all of this. In my footloose and fancy-free status, I had envisioned presents, letters and language declaring love and life for me from the prince of my life. In actuality, I am finding out how unreal and restricted I would feel if that were to happen. There would be no actual basis for such promises. We are at best friendly strangers who do not "belong" to each other.

Well in any case, I have quietly absorbed all the information that has come my way in the last months and have reciprocated as thoroughly and authentically as I could. I have thought of November and evaded any possibilities. In this state, I called Abraham yesterday to inform him on a question he had about medicine here. We talked briefly in reference to our letters, and I made the comment about how I wondered if he was telling me the truth about his gourmet cooking. He replied that he rather enjoyed cooking and asked if I had a problem with this. I replied in the negative. He went on to ask if I had any problem marrying him? I was thrown off by the impromptu question. My response was equally impromptu. I replied a jellylike "no." There was no time to ponder on the momentousness of his question and my response. He reworded his question, "Would you like to marry me?" Very much in the mode of my drowning moments in Kenya, I said, "yes." I suspect that at some unconscious level I must have known that I had little reason to reject him. He replied that he would make me "the happiest wife." I had neither the integrity nor the courage to tell him likewise. Instead, I just said, "I'll *try* to do my best." Even as I write this, I know that that telephonic exchange was purely a matter of sheer dumb, blind *faith*. Nothing less, nothing more; any rationale here defies all reason. I called my parents. They were subdued and grateful for the news. I called you and you were away gallivanting. The wedding will be sometime after Christmas. I hope you will come to be in it. No doubt, I hardly know what all of this means. I am more numb by all that is overtaking me. Very, very different from what I had imagined for myself.

People ask me if I love this man: "Are you in love?" I answer with a "no." They are visibly disturbed. This will be a journey of grace, trust and discovery (like most other journeys, really). While one must do all one can to affect the course and the outcome in such matters, at the end of the day there are no guarantees. We are all such inexact creatures. Time will tell. This holds true regardless of one's culture.

This language of "love" in the culture of romance is also fraught with potential difficulties. Far too much hangs on that peg. In my last letter I had written to you about the significance (for me, anyhow) of abstaining from physical involvement in courtship. Equally problematic are the semantics of romance. While it appears that language and physical affection as they relate to courtship have the potential to reduce the "terror of the unknown" that I am going through, they also become mechanisms of foreclosure whereby outcomes to the relationship are predetermined. What do I mean? Like all the kisses and the hand-holdings, the "I love you's," the "disconcertingly lovely" and "madly in love" bits also steer the direction of the relationship, taking away control from the individuals them-selves. As you have alluded to in one of your earlier letters, your attention is captured when someone has declared his attrac-tion/affection to you. Profound emotions expressed through words can have a binding effect on you. You spin the wheel then and hope that you get lucky.

Besides the *nature* of courtship, the *duration* of courtship in the West is yet another potentially influential factor in the outcome of the relationship. I have noticed that short courtships can lead to hasty decisions (especially with young people), while long courtships can lead to too much investment that makes divest-ment harder. All in all, courtship appears tantamount to mar-riage itself in form and substance. Every time I go to a Western wedding, I am struck by all the sweet ceremonial rhetoric of trust, hope and commitment, when in fact these vows had been exchanged much earlier on in the courtship. Where are the ele-ments of discovery, newness, even fear, trust, obedience and betrothal that people experience in the Eastern context? It appears that there is a far greater degree of control and rational-ity for the couple in the West. In part these are the conse-quences of social changes that have found it necessary to dismantle social control and regulation in order to pursue indi-vidual choice and freedom. My own feeling is that an alterna-tive ethic of courtship could be useful for freer choices.

Hence it is very difficult for me to engage in the language of love with regards to Abraham. This has little to do with any reaction on my part to forms of romance in the West. It is more deep-seated than that. This willingness to give this man a chance, to write to him and then say yes last night comes about from something deep within that I revisited that night on the train. I have learnt that so much I held on to obsessively and compulsively was quite irrelevant in the larger scheme of our lives. Life is very short. This is perhaps what Abraham means when he says that he can make do with any two shirts. Our challenge is to live it the best way we know. Partnerships are good if this perspective can be shared and pursued. That is all. I hope to grow to love this man. *Love* is still not the word though. It is about something more dynamic and open-ended, and perhaps even something less, something more modest and real than all the utopian aspirations present in the cadences of romance. For me it is about faith, respect, sharing and caring, knowing all along that nothing belongs to you, not even yourself. We are on loan here. I feel an element of obedience here, a call to honour something bigger than myself. Perhaps it has to do with the conviction that the realm of the personal is enormously implicated with that of the public, and I hope to honour that. Equally, the single state is hugely implicated in this commitment to do the work of God. One only has to consider Jesus.

I do not want you to get the impression that I have resigned myself to fate. In one sense we all are, in all our cultures. For me it is about pursuing "abundance within limits"—the limits of mortality. I believe that these days in particular I have been forced to take a look at some of the "existential" limits I operate under.

I am frightened. Abraham could turn out to be a complete impostor. I can only trust that he has been to me what I have been to him—honest. If I should be sadly surprised, I hope for grace and wisdom then. Until then, I am trusting God to honour my feeble attempt at faithfulness.

I don't have much more to say. I will be in touch.

Soberly yours,
Ivy

Renegotiating Romance

England: November 15th, 1989

Dear Ivy,

Many thanks for your last two letters. I am delighted that you have decided to marry Abraham. Even in this decision, I am impressed by the absence of the kind of hype that would probably accompany such a decision here in the West. The Proposal. The Engagement. It all goes along with the champagne and red roses and weepy violins and soft-focus photographs that are the accompanying chords of Romantic Love.

Yet, there is deep gladness and great joy at your decision. I am honoured that you have asked me to be your bridesmaid. I will certainly be there by your side. I realised how disappointed I would have been had the whole thing come to naught during the time when you seemed to be waiting so long for Abraham's first letter. I was immensely relieved to discover that it was a hitch in the postal service and not the courtship! In retrospect, I can imagine that the waiting and not being sure on both sides might have provided a space for each of you to consider the prospect of a life without the other. No doubt it was a good test of whether or not there is indeed growing affection. And yet I am struck by your refusal to weigh this more heavily than you ought. Such a different way of courtship from the West!

Your comments about not seeing Abraham again before making your decision were very interesting. If you repudiate the qualification of "being in love" with its dependence on "chemistry" and physical attraction, a further meeting was of course redundant. You have had the opportunity to get to know each other by letter, and no doubt this offers a more straightforward way of finding out about someone's real concerns and values than a few highly charged meetings might accomplish.

Yet, you are still clearly wanting to exercise your individuality in this "getting to know." Your past twenty years have shown that you are not willing to marry just anyone who is the right religion, age, class and education. Your choosing involves quite a detailed "getting to know," albeit at a distance and without the time spent in each other's company in the process. You are determined to find value in qualities which our sex-obsessed, in-love-dependent Western culture too often misses: humility, self-sacrificial caring, acquaintance with suffering, and love for the world. And I admit that attention to these more enduring qualities is too often submerged under the "chemistry" that may often be no more than lust in Western courtship. The whole rhetoric of "falling in love" is very complex and very seductive and offers a notoriously flimsy grounding for any attempt at lifelong partnership.

Indeed, your last two letters, perhaps more than any previously, have made me think a great deal about our respective ways of going about this whole business of finding a partner. The two questions that have preoccupied you—what good would have come from seeing him again, and are you in love—have given me food for thought too. They stem from assumptions about what courtship involves in the West, and I find myself stopped in my tracks when challenged by the possibility that the answers to them are not inevitable.

And yet the Eastern way is not possible for us. Courtship with barely any meeting is not really an option for young Westerners, and a relationship which refrains from any kind of physical touch before marriage is also an unlikely prospect for most. Boys and girls, men and women are not so rigorously differentiated in the West as they are in the East. And no doubt this is, as is true for all cultural norms, deeply ambivalent with potential for both liberation and entrapment. It means there is greater flexibility in gender roles—women presumably have a greater range of opportunities open to them than would be possible in a more rigidly stratified and segregated society. But the negative aspects of a less regulated set of conventions between the sexes—really quite recent in the West—are also drastically limiting in their ways—as you and I have already explored. I have found it much harder than you to negotiate close friendship between myself as a single woman and Joel, a married man. Indeed relationship between any two people of the opposite sex—or even the same sex—is more problematic in our more free-floating, fast-changing, boundary-blurring culture. There is much more likelihood of ambiguity, of playing games, of leading people on, of hurt and confusion and broken hearts.

And as teachers and confidantes, you and I have seen at first hand some of the ways in which young people of the West are hurt in the course of "relationship" procedures here. Even young Christians, who are taught to question the dictates of their culture when it comes to sexual ethics, often struggle. You and I have both listened to students, confident that they are being Christian in their courtship just because they stop short of actual intercourse before the wedding night, and each of us has helped to mop up the tears and recriminations when such relationships do not work out—and then watched in helpless trepidation when the round starts all over again. This failure to take seriously the bonds of the body, as well as the way that touch does have the capacity to push a relationship too fast and too inevitably down one track, comes from a kind of Western dualism that seems endemic in this latter part of the twentieth century.

Yet touch, as you say, can no longer mean for us what it does for you in your culture. Had a potential suitor of mine not immediately put out a hand to rescue me if I was about to fall down a pothole, I would have been disappointed and taken it as a sign of his lack of consideration and manners. And in a culture like mine, where the sexes have been mingling since childhood, there is no doubt a much greater sense of casualness towards touching someone of the opposite sex. (This may well be a very recent phenomenon; I know that my grandmother's approach to courtship was much closer to yours than it is to mine.) Indeed, our taboos in the West are more to do with same-sex touching. A friend once told me that men walk down the street hand in hand in India without a hint of self-consciousness. Here, some sort of sexual liaison would immediately be suspected.

What should I make of these different meanings for touch? As with so many things, my feelings are mixed. The possibilities in my culture seem both liberating and limiting. I know that even some of my Christian friends are amazed at my desire to stick to the old-fashioned value of no sex before marriage. To them it seems repressive, oppressive and suggests that one is making too big a deal of sex. Some have assured me that, having waited so long, that when it comes, sex will be a big disappointment. But that's not really the point. It seems that I want to retain the freedom for the sexual act to mean something quite important, a kind of ultimate self-giving to another. I suppose this is something close to what I think marriage is all about. I also don't believe them when they say that sex is no big deal. This kind of protestation leaves me far from convinced. How does one explain, then, its almost unrivaled power to hurt when a loved one is unfaithful? Such pain surely gives the lie to the dualism by which we try to live.

I remember, years ago, long before I knew you existed, watching a documentary about different perspectives on marriage throughout the world. In particular, I recall the diametrically contrasting examples of a Californian couple and an Indian couple. The Californian couple had an "open marriage," and during the course of the interview, the husband made the startling claim that "It doesn't matter what I do with my body; my heart is always faithful to my wife." I was astounded by such a dislocation between body and self. By contrast, the Indian man, when asked on his wedding day by an incredulous Western documentary maker who told us that this man had not seen the woman he was about to marry, "But do you love your wife?", gave the most beautiful smile and said, "I *will* love her." Even then, it struck me that this was far closer to the Christian understanding of love than any of the other perspectives, even though a number of the other worldviews presented on this program had supposedly evolved from the Christian tradition.

And yet again, I know that such nostalgia on my part is not enough. The way of that Indian couple in the documentary, of you and Abraham, even the way of my grandmother—the Scottish way of seventy years ago—is not open to me. I am both more free and more unfree. It is not that our system is any more inherently flawed than yours. Surely in the arranged marriage setup there is just as much potential for violence done to individuals as there is in the Western market of free love. And surely would-be cultural dissidents in the West, whilst unable to live outside their culture, and inevitably shaped by it for both good and ill, can yet do their best to resist those aspects of it which run counter to the gospel of love. Physical contact (and by this I mean nonsexual touch) before marriage does not inevitably lead to a kind of compulsive slide to the altar, just as the absence of premarriage physical contact in the East is no guarantee that the marriage will be genuinely supportive to both partners. There are many marriages I know here in the West that are rooted in the very qualities that you are seeking in your marriage with Abraham. These give me hope that it is, after all, possible to negotiate one's culture and find a better way, like you have, within it.

It is surely possible for Christians and other dissidents to learn from all this, for us to discover through dialogue with others the idols of our culture that we are too close to identify for ourselves. I suppose it is in this spirit, as well as in the spirit of friendship, that I am so interested in following your story as it unfolds, and so glad to be taken into your confidence. It is indeed a challenge; but were I to believe that the Western way per se was utterly doomed, then I would be sunk indeed!

But enough of this. You have other important letters to read, and I am eager to hear how the courtship is going. I'll phone you at the weekend to discuss wedding dates and plans. What on earth do I wear? I've never been a bridesmaid at an Indian wedding before! (And don't expect me to wear a saree! It would look ridiculous on me, with my long back and large expanse of incredibly white midriff!)

Love,
M.

Renegotiating Friendship

Dear Ivy,

How hard it has been to return to cold and dreary England! I am feeling very low right now, no doubt a mixture of jet lag, the beginnings of a cold, the anticlimax after all the excitement of the months leading up to your wedding, and the anticipation of getting back into harness for what promises to be a very hard term ahead after an idyllic three weeks in India. I can't quite believe that only a week ago, I was lolling in the Arabian Sea, watching the sun set gloriously over the Goan horizon. Like so many, I fell in love with India and was so glad to have the chance to get to know a little of your country, even though I was sad to be exploring it without you.

It was certainly a very different experience traveling around with another Westerner after the first week spent with you in your parents' home in Madras. I am grateful for the more intimate glimpse of India your family offered me. As soon as I left you all after the wedding, I felt very much the tourist, defined only by my white skin and potential spending power. Yet it was still an incredible experience, and I carry a thousand and one vivid images of your diverse and confounding land.

It stirred up in me many of my childhood memories of Africa: the colour, the heat, the smells, the diversity, the countless, nameless villages we passed on the train, the waving large-bellied children, the extremes of wealth and poverty. It has left me disconcerted, and no doubt this has something to do with my present mood. How I wish I could talk to you right now! It was hard coming back to the UK because my sense of "home" has been unsettled by all the deep-rooted, primary memories of Africa stirred up by your own subcontinent! For the first time in years, returning to Britain did not feel for me much like a homecoming.

But there is something else that I realise is dragging me down. It's a nagging feeling of loss, the small, tormenting voice that asks me every so often: have I lost my best friend? Has your marriage set a chasm between us so that now I must negotiate and tread diplomatically where once I could move boldly and take so much for granted? Even the question of phoning you: what if I am interrupting something? (OK, as a sex-obsessed single Westerner, you can guess my assumptions). I know that you will not misunderstand me when I talk about this sense of bereavement; I suppose the fact that I can even write this shows that at some level I don't really believe that anything fundamental has been lost.

Yet we have lost our common status as two single friends together, laughing and scheming and taking for granted a certain kindred and kinship and freedom in our single status. It's strange, this new stage. I thought it was odd when a number of our friends would ask, when they learned of your impending marriage, how I felt about it. It seemed then a nonquestion: very happy, of course. But now I begin to feel some of the shades of what they meant, the shadow of doubt, the flicker of nervousness that something has died between us forever.

But I am being melancholy, in true Celtic style. You and I have talked about this on a number of occasions. And here again, I am aware that the fact that you are Indian makes a difference. I think that for many Western women, marriage does indeed feel as if it takes away their former soulmates. It's not that this phenomenon does not exist in India; indeed, you have told me yourself how after your childhood friends married it was as if a blanket dropped between yourself and them. But I think that was about something a little different, maybe more to do with the fact that you were mystified by their compliance in an arrangement which, at that stage, you found incomprehensible.

For Westerners it is a different set of issues. Because we tend to assume that the marriage partner will also be our best friend—indeed our expectations of what one other limited individual can supply by way of our emotional needs is doubtless catastrophically high—there is the possibility that other friends feel somewhat "dropped" when a serious relationship with someone of the opposite sex takes off. It is part of the pattern I mentioned ages ago, that female friends can too easily be seen as temporary companions with whom to tread the water—until one can really get on with the true job of human relating and intimacy. I have also noticed that married friends move through this phase of absorption and then realise that their husband is not, after all, enough. They still need other forms of intimacy, and their attention drifts back to their neglected friends. I paint this scenario somewhat harshly.

Yet it is no doubt that this realisation, working almost at a subliminal level, is part of what is feeding this slight sense of depression and displacement in me. And yet I really do feel that with us this is far from inevitable. Your whole way of approaching marriage has been so very different from any I have experienced before. You have not been swept away in a tide of Romantic Love, and there is none of the expectation that Abraham will be Everything to you. There is none of the high rhetoric, and none of the consequent sense on my part that I am now redundant. No doubt one of the very positive values of marriage in your culture is this avoidance of placing the other too much at centre stage, the assumption that the network of women's friendships and other communal obligations are not superseded by the new tie. I know that from now on, I cannot be your primary point of reference. Abraham, to use a Western idiom, is now the "significant other." But that does not render me insignificant.

As you will see, I am drawing comfort from rehearsing these assurances to myself that I know you would offer yourself, were you on the other end of the phone or computer. But by now you will be coming to the end of the Andamans honeymoon. I look forward to hearing from you how it all went, and how married life is going. I suppose there is more suspense involved in this question when the couple have only been together for eleven hours before they meet at the altar.

Ivy, I have been thinking a great deal about our time together in India. It was so good to meet your family, having heard so much about them for these last years: your frail but indomitable mother, so full of thankfulness to God that at last her wayward daughter had complied, and bending over backwards not to do anything that might offend and threaten a marriage that she must have dreamed of for so long, and feared for almost as long would never come to pass. Your dear father, simply content to have you near. Now I see at first hand where you get your confidence and reassurance, what with such a great-souled and mighty mother and an unselfconsciously adoring father! And although they are many worlds away, how much they reminded me of my own family. Maybe it is that they are of the same generation, and so many of our assumptions have to do with our place in history rather than our place in culture. But no doubt my sense of the kinship was also because I feel as if I know them so well through you and perhaps the insides of families are not so very different the world over—only so many combinations of tensions and issues and relationships.

One of my most vivid memories before the wedding was both of us waking up in the middle of the night on Christmas morning, our bodies still working to a very different clock. Both too hot to sleep, and you in a cold sweat about what you had let yourself in for, we embarked on a walk, for what seemed like hours through the streets of Madras, gradually wending our way toward the cathedral. I remember the friendly greetings from the few fellows who passed us on their bicycles: "Merry Christmas!" they would shout to me in delight at having met someone so early in the day who, with her white skin and Western garb would be bound to be impressed with such a greeting. But even more, I remember your sense of near panic when you awoke. What if he turned out to be a psychopath like that cat killer who once crossed your path? What if he was cruel to you? What if you were miserable? If you had let yourself in for a lifetime of unhappiness? For a minute or two I wondered if you would indeed lose your nerve and be unable to go through with it. How good it was to be there, to remind you of his kindness right from the start, his consideration for your feelings, your dilemma, the long letters, the reports from all who knew him and his family. As the night dissipated, so did your fears....

Until you were about to meet him again. There we waited in our room in Bangalore, painting our toenails as a means of whiling away the time before the meeting alone between you and him—specially negotiated between me and his mischievous brother. Do you remember the knock on the door, us leaping into the air, the scarlet varnish almost spilled all over the floor in our nervousness at the impending meeting? Like two schoolgirls awaiting the first date. Which is what it was like in a way, but with staggeringly more at stake! Have you asked Abraham yet what he made of us when he came in, me hastily excusing myself only to be discovered by him five minutes later at the bottom of the stairs, painting the remaining toenails a rather wobbly red?

From then on, it seemed the most natural thing in the world, the wedding in that jasmine-bedecked cathedral, the colourful sarees, the glorious sunshine streaming in through the open side doors, the incredible Indian feast to follow. And yet it was like no wedding I have been at before. I suppose for me, as for you, it represented a journey which has caused me to ponder so many questions about human intimacy and relating. Reading the love chapter from 1 Corinthians 13 took on a new significance as I read it on your wedding day in that cathedral in Bangalore. The choosing to love, the commitment to love, the whole vocabulary of love that lay behind that Indian man in the documentary sweetly saying of his stranger bride, "I *will* love her," all this came into focus. And for all this, I am extremely grateful.

It leaves me thinking, wondering about the implications of all of this for me. How one grapples with one's culture, wresting from it its good inheritances, trying to negotiate, even on occasion redeem, what is damaged or damaging. I still have a long way to go, but were I to start considering a serious relationship again, I really do believe that my starting points would not be what they once were.

Ivy, write as soon as you can. Give my love to Abraham, and make sure you are good to that husband of yours. Remember to remind him: if you fight, I'm on his side!

Love,
M.

New Realities

Boston: January 24th, 1990

Dear Margaret:

Greetings! We are back from our honeymoon, back from saying farewells to our families in India and now, after the activity and movement and the sense of being on a helter-skelter, we are settling into new rhythms here in the U.S. The memory of your part in the wedding and your visit to India will always remain with me. Your presence by my side at the altar for me symbolised God's presence in my aloneness. It was reassuring in light of my terrible anguish in Amsterdam last summer.

The ceremonial rituals were a reminder that no one was saying "I do"; rather it was a "we do." I was not alone. At that time I understood that I was marrying into a family, a people, a story, a memory beyond ourselves. I was especially pleased that I could substitute "heed" for "obey" in my vows, thanks to Abraham's warning me ahead of time. While the wedding ceremony and reception were full of garlands of all fragrances and colours, I had the real sense that God had come to garland me that day, and I took the courage to bow down in honour. We had a lovely week in the Andamans afterwards.

You ask how is married life? I don't know how to answer that. In many ways life is no different from before; little has altered. As you know the adjustments have all been on Abraham's side. Quitting the cigarette after twenty years, leaving his post in India, coming here to join me, etc. While it is still early days, I suspect that these days are a forerunner of our days to come.

I am struck by the uncomplicated man that Abraham is. There is an essential quality about him that is reliable. He is a devoted man and an independent man. I put it this way because while on the one hand I occupy a central place in his universe, I am not so central that he will not go on without me. That is freeing. He is a humble man who senses God closely. The other day I heard him pray, "Thank you for the faith that you will ultimately deliver us from evil." I too face the future with that faith.

In concrete and palpable ways, our worlds (of teaching and medicine) are so radically different, affording a certain richness and variety. I cannot tell you enough of the immense joys of shared language, food, stories, etc., that we enter into so naturally (I realise how significant this is for an expatriate). He adds fullness to my being. He is housebroken in astonishing ways—a superb cook, very well organised, etc. Thanks are largely due to his parents. I probably drive him crazy with my wayward ways.

What is this marriage doing *to* me? At the level of first-order questions, life with Abraham is no different from the loving home I grew up in. There is security and assurance. I never dreamed it would be so. In fact that is one of the reasons I put off marriage—no one less than my father and no place less than my home would do. At the level of the second order, I am struck by something more profound, something constant, a lesson for the very first time really—it has to do with the love of God. I am quite incapable of putting it into words for fear that I will cheapen the truth.

You and I have always been told about the love of God and our responsive love for God. Lifelong, we have been given all sorts of motifs to illustrate this, and we have in turn tried to order our lives around this. In my case I cannot quite give you an explanation of this truth except in the incarnational story of Jesus; even then I would assign a special significance to this truth claiming that it was about Jesus, an extraordinary being.

The love of my family I always took for granted and did not read any special meaning into it. It is with Abraham that I am seeing anew the meaning of God's obsession with us. Abraham cares for me deeply and freely, and I have no other option but to care back. Speaking about caring freely, while I made a big issue of all the life changes that would come upon me as a result of this new relationship, I have been pleasantly surprised. He is big enough to be gracious to my other "loves"—you and other attachments. He humbles me—convicting me with his own generosity.

Margaret, ours (yours and mine) has been a special union. This was why I was so fearful of losing you. We have shared so much. As you have so often said, together we've been very lucky. We have been free people, eager to affirm each other and wanting the most for one another (in my case to a fault almost). This friendship has been like no other. I think of so much we have done together. Our travels—remember our evening drive to Stonehenge and trespassing there; do you also remember that night at the theatre, watching the Fugard play and how at the end we managed to get actor John Kani to pose with us, only to find out later that the camera had no film? I was so cross with myself. Serves me right though! I think of our holidays—remember how you left the giblets in the first turkey you cooked? Our innumerable meals together—the crisps and M & S sandwiches at your end, and all the Indian food at mine! All our unending conversations, the books, the clothes and the music we gave each other, the way I have taken to your family as my own, the fun we had with Aunt Margaret, blind as she was. So much! My friends still talk about the spark in me when I refer to you! We entered each other's worlds so effortlessly, almost as if destined. More than anything of course has been our faith in

God. Sorry, I don't mean to wax nostalgic. These are substantive sentiments that have been formative to my being, and I am deeply grateful. No doubt from a practical standpoint the future will transform our present intensities, but you will always remain a vital part of my life.

So, regarding your own concerns about our continuing friendship. Well before the wedding I told Abraham that you were part of my dowry, that you would go with me where I went. He appeared nonplussed, not knowing what the issue was all about, as if to say, "I don't understand how this marriage can affect that friendship." I need not have worried that he would be possessive or unsupportive. In any case I have also known that marriage relationships cannot be self-sufficient without a whole world of support outside. I have never understood how one can make a radical break between past and present. So the challenge really is up to you to get up the gumption to call/come anytime.

The joy of body and language (my references in previous letters) in the marriage take on altogether different connotations from those outside it. They are not tools of power and desire misjudged as "love." Rather these expressions are free and purposeful with little "lost" but much that is continually and exponentially added.

Margaret, in the end I have been given a gift. One takes no credit for gifts. For all the caution that I have exercised, I realise that it could have gone so badly wrong, as it has in so many lives. I can only say that I tried. I am deeply grateful to my culture for providing me with some structures to appropriate this gift. I am so glad that I left India to return to embrace the wisdom of that which I had earlier considered foolish. I am also aware that this is only one gift among many. Marriage is not the end. There is another end yet—the End of embracing the delicate web of life and moving on as creatures towards God. In this understanding there's room for all sorts of us—singles, spares, marrieds, odds and ends, all God's bits of work. We are both aware of this when we say our hellos and good-byes daily.

Gandhi suggested that as an exercise towards a nonviolent world, it would be helpful if people could carve out territories of nonviolence in their own lives. In other words, individuals should demarcate areas in their daily lives (family, marriage, special relationships, neighbourhood, work, etc.) as unequivocally sacrosanct, which would then move them along towards the larger goal of human transformation. As I think about it, I want to declare this marriage as being such a space. Of course, as with every noble goal, this too stands subject to human corruptibility. Not infrequently, we see spouses who are uncritical apologists of what appear to be unhealthy marriage relationships. Such folk block any possibility for critical transformation of self and other. By "sacrosanct" I don't mean a display of chauvinism towards one's marriage. Rather, what I mean is that in this space one is left with work to do. The work of self-transformation, the work of trothkeeping, the work of prayer, the work of love, the work of discipline and patience, the work of giving, the work of gratitude and celebration. Here lies the gift dimension of this relationship and an opportunity to demonstrate how one might set out to multiply such spaces and commitments in the public sphere as well. My friendship with you is also one such space for me.

I don't know if there is such a thing as a "planned" life, but I do believe in "examined" lives. Again I don't know if one can deliberate "examination." While leaving India was probably one of the most tortuous experiences for me, I feel as if I was forced off the road to take my place in a lay-by while all the other traffic whizzed past me. My static status drove me to understand the highly social nature of this institution of marriage. One does not have to marry. Many single people can speak to this truth. I saw that because of social factors, marriage forms varied from people to people and from age to age. In this sense, East is not far from West historically with regards to marriage. You have told me about the standards for selection of a mate in your grandparents' time—able-bodied and hardworking. This is not very different from many Indian agricultural communities today. So also, polygamy, polyandry, arranged marriages are all relative to time, place and people without being endemic to any.

My challenge all these years has been to sort out what in my system has been life-giving and to negotiate the rest. I know that I am deeply grateful for a later marriage. It was a most lucky escape, I feel. Fifteen years ago, I hardly knew my own person, and I have lived through sea changes in my worldviews since then. Unlike in an earlier time, the farm, my family property, their lineage, etc., did not depend on my marriage. Only I depended on it and I had the choice. This was an important lesson. Similarly, all this talk of the "biological" clock in females is largely a "social" clock. Again, with children as with marriage, one does not *have* to have children. For better and for worse, the world today is in a different place.

An unintentional life can be a real loss. What I have learnt in this short while of marriage is that it pays a great deal to think through much of what we have been brought up to see as "inevitable." I have often speculated on the course of my life had I not come West. Who knows? As hard as all these years have been, quite often I knew that I had taken as much existential charge of my life as I could. I didn't often feel that this was possible when I was home. I suspect that this is the case for a lot of people. But I don't believe that one *has* to leave one's home to engage in introspection, to take stock of the significant and the lasting. The roster of human experience is rife with the lives of great souls, women and men who in their inherited spaces mustered up the moral will to resist and who sought the abandon of life's wild dances.

As I reflect on the imperative of an intentional life, one other sobering insight comes to me on the matter. It has to do with how much the state of the public sphere contributes to the personal. The totality of the material circumstances in the surrounding society contributes a great deal to fostering individual ideals and values—far more than we know. Hence, my ability to choose has all along been afforded to me by my relative enjoyment of economic, political and social stability in my public world. In periods of prolonged crises such as poverty, fascism, slavery, apartheid, war, and cultural turmoil, appropriate ethical engagement in one's life choices are quickly aborted. Writers like Toni Morrison and Nadine Gordimer have pointed this out. So I am constantly aware that my options were never really viable options for so many others. The present-day globalisation of economies and cultures is I fear one such mitigating circumstance in terms of individual choice and freedom.

So take your time my dear, try to listen to the dissonance in you. And I promise not to do to you what others have perhaps inadvertently done to me: to ask, "Why are *you* not married?" I hope that this gives you some sense of the life and times of yours truly. Look forward to being in touch soon.

Love,
Ivy

CONCLUSION

Ivy George

And so ends a chapter in the lives of two friends. What are we to make of it all? This book was never on our minds: in many ways it was pried out of us by friends and relations who were privy to our correspondences. It represents a small segment of a bountiful friendship. As the reader knows by now, we were and are in the habit of letters, phone calls and visits. When circumstances in both our lives inspired us to bring our two hearts and heads together in negotiating each other's "passages" of that time, these letters came about.

Our point of closure and conclusion of this work with my marriage was utterly pragmatic, and we hope that it does not stand as a distraction to the goals of the larger discussion. While the "happily ever after" idea of human relations is contrary to both our sensibilities, the incident of my marriage offered a convenient transition point for our conversations until then. Our hopes for ourselves and others have been to explore our potential for personal and social transformation as it is played out in our private lives.

Some years back, Gail Sheehy wrote, "There are only two or three human stories. And they go on repeating themselves as fiercely as if they never happened before." We recognise the universality of the underlying themes of our exchanges: our stories and the questions to which they give rise are thus not new or original. Yet we know also that these are particular stories of particular times. The changing nature of culture is such that the distinctions between East and West are more in terms of time than in essence, for in an earlier time the communities in the West also displayed patterns of social relationships similar to those of traditional communities in the East. Thus the idea of arranged marriages was once not as alien in Western life as it sounds in our age today, and the culture of romance was not always as commonplace as it seems.

This project was carried out with the recognition that human intimacy is a gift, a blessing. In our exchanges about intimacy and meaningful relations, we have been moved by a quest for the significance of our choices. We have been made aware that our choices affect not only ourselves, but as concentrically located selves they affect even more deeply the world outside us and its future. For after all, in our everyday choices and relations we are unwittingly telling one another the kind of world we want to shape and live in. Here our understanding of a "covenantal" relationship as being two dimensional has been influential in our explorations. A covenant between God and self expresses itself inevitably at the lateral level between one's self and one's community of participation and accountability. In the most intimate of one's relations, one stands as a witness of hope for others around one and the generations to come.

Inasmuch as persons, groups and social institutions influence private and public life, cross-cultural discourse is highly significant in the negotiation of tradition and modernity for postmodern life in our time. A project such as ours may be valuable for this reason. For each of us, our expatriate status and cross-cultural friendship have been of immense significance. In this work, our own story is incidental; there may be incidents, experiences, moments of insight that our readers may well recognise as carrying echoes of their own stories. But it is a wider and more general recognition that we hope we have conveyed here. Because our thinking spans two cultures with rather different approaches to human intimacy, each of us has been pushed into an awareness of our respective situations in new and more immediate ways.

As a migrant who dwells in the interstices of the East and West, I am consciousness of the resources extant in our various cultural traditions. Increasingly, societies outside the West are giving way to the cultures of modernity and new conceptions of freedom are regularly introduced. It is unfortunate that the dynamic of such change is often linear, where the new dominates the old and the old is forever erased. Yet, surely it may not be as final as that. I am struck by the highly porous nature of cultures and the regenerative capacities within and between them. There lie in every culture submerged possibilities for constructive human transformation. In order to ferret out these possibilities within oneself and one's surrounding culture, being at one remove as a cultural dissident and critic is important. It starts by recognising that the forces of culture are highly influential in our thoughts on the matter. The culture of romance emerges as the apotheosis of modernity and seems to be the only available script, and many are hopelessly bound by its power. There hardly seems any space or support to ponder the virtues of singleness and celibacy in a sexually saturated cultural climate. Those who dare to be independent-minded are relegated to dysfunctional status. Yet, the exercise of an alternative ethic in intimate relationships can be immensely liberating.

We close acknowledging that from the outset we have known that this is a "high-risk" project. In such an enterprise, there is ample room for indulgence, self-advertisement and self-importance, and doubtless we have not always escaped these ourselves. Indeed, this work has been the result of a relationship between two particular women, with all the attendant particularities that emerge from the encasements of our respective biographies, our distinctive social and historical contexts. Quite possibly our questions about "relationship" are nonquestions for many in these shifting times. We are well aware of this reality from our involvements with men and women in our work in higher education. While this might be the case, we still hope that our questions and our responses can be kept alive among all who view the conversation as a small contribution to the quest for models of sustainable relationships in humane cultures.

THE END